Place Value

Name ______________________________

Dizzy Digits

Read the clues and write each number described.

1. It has 9 digits. All the digits are 0 except one 6. What is the number?

____

2. If you reverse the digits on this three-digit number, it will have 4 hundreds, 9 tens, and 7 ones. What is the original number?

____

3. The digits of this number are in sequential order. If you add the four digits together, they add up to 10. None of the digits are zero. What is the number?

____

4. List all the different four-digit numbers that use the digits 4, 4, 5, and 5.

____

5. All the digits are the same in this five-digit number. The sum of the digits is 30. What is the number?

____

6. Use each of the digits 1 through 8 to make two four-digit numbers. Arrange to give the greatest possible sum when the two numbers are added together.

____

7. If you reverse the digits on this five-digit number, it will have 9 ten-thousands, 4 thousands, 8 hundreds, and 1 one. What is the number?

____

8. List the different numbers that are possible, using these clues. The number of hundreds plus the number of thousands is 2. The number of tens is 3 times the number of thousands. The number of ones is 2 times the number of hundreds.

____

9. Write the largest five-digit number possible using any digits 1 through 9. No digit may be used more than once.

____

Addition

With Renaming

Name ______________________

The Great Calorie Count

Everyone in Marjorie's family counted calories to maintain a healthy weight. Read about their meals and write the number of calories calculated.

1. Marjorie made a sandwich for her school lunch. She used 2 slices of bread at 58 calories each. She spread 1 tablespoon of margarine on the bread at 101 calories. She added 1 slice of cheese at 101 calories, and a slice of lunch meat at 161 calories. How many calories were in her sandwich?

   ____

2. Along with her sandwich, Marjorie ate a pear with 101 calories. She also bought a half-pint of milk with 152 calories. How many calories were in her whole lunch?

   ____

3. Her brother George packed his lunch with two chicken legs with 209 calories each, a container of applesauce at 116 calories, a celery stick at 7 calories and a cookie at 96 calories. How many calories were in George's lunch?

   ____

4. For breakfast, Marjorie, her brother, and her parents each had a dish of oatmeal at 130 calories, a glass of milk at 150 calories, and a half-cup of raisins at 210 calories. How many breakfast calories did they all have together?

   ____

5. For dinner, each family member ate a serving of roast beef at 393 calories, corn on the cob at 242 calories, with margarine at 101 calories. They had green beans at 17 calories, a salad at 52 calories, with dressing at 41 calories. They each had a glass of milk at 150 calories. Their mother said they could have dessert if they each stayed under 1,000 calories for the whole meal. Will they get dessert? Explain.

   ____

6. For dessert they each had chocolate ice cream at 220 calories and a slice of cake with 320 calories. How many calories were in each dessert?

   ____

7. How many calories did Marjorie eat today for breakfast, lunch, and dinner combined?

   ____

USE YOUR CALCULATOR

How many total calories did the four people in Marjorie's family eat for dinner and dessert?

____

Addition

With Regrouping

Name ______________________

When I Grow Up

The upper grades at Glenridge School were studying different jobs. Speakers at a job fair taught them about the costs involved in various jobs. Calculate the costs described.

1. Louis's father came to talk about his music store. He showed the students a saxophone for \$719.95, a clarinet for \$859.95, and a flute for \$825.95. If the school band bought all three instruments, how much would they spend?

   ____

2. Bob's mother is a photographer. She brought in her equipment and talked about events she had photographed. She described one job for which she spent \$60 for film, \$75 for developing the film, and \$85 in other expenses. How much did it cost her to photograph that event?

   ____

3. David's father, a traveling salesman, flies to different cities to sell his products. In one month he flew to Atlanta for \$239, to New Orleans for \$349, and to Dallas for \$431. How much did he have to spend on airfare that month?

   ____

4. Tim's mother is a landscaper. On a new home in the neighborhood, she spent \$829 for trees, \$358 for flowers, and \$352 for a fish pond. How much did she spend on items for the new yard?

   ____

5. The children asked their teacher, Mr. Thompson, if he had any expenses. He explained that, among other things, he took a class last summer. It cost him \$515 for tuition, \$49 for a book, and \$29 for other expenses (pens, paper, etc.). How much did Mr. Thompson spend for summer school?

   ____

6. Tori's father, a policeman, came to school to talk about his job. The students asked him to list some of his expenses. He spent \$239 for a uniform, \$219 for his gun, \$198 for his jacket, and \$49 for his handcuffs. How much did it cost to outfit himself?

   ____

7. Beverly's father is an auto repairman. When he visited, he said that his expenses included tools, which cost \$2,500, a cart to slide under the cars for \$149, and \$59 for his uniform. What was the total of these expenses?

   ____

USE YOUR CALCULATOR

The students made a book detailing the expenses of various jobs. The students spent \$17 on paper for the book, \$25 on magic markers, and \$3 for pencils. What was the total of their expenses?

____

They produced 25 copies of the book with those supplies. What was the average cost of each book?

____

Subtraction

With Renaming

Name ______________________________

Meet Me at the Fair

In 1904, the world's fair in St. Louis caused much wonder among people. New inventions, foods, and art sparked interest throughout the world. Read about the fair and calculate the problems.

1. Peanut butter was introduced at the world's fair in 1904. The first commercial peanut butter was produced by a St. Louis doctor in 1890. How long after its production was it introduced at the fair?

   ____

2. The largest Ferris wheel was built for the Chicago Fair in 1893. The same Ferris wheel was used at the St. Louis world's fair in 1904, then torn down and sold for scrap in 1904. How many years did the Ferris wheel run?

   ____

3. No one is sure where ice cream was first made, but the ice cream cone was first used at the world's fair in 1904. How many years has it been since we first used the cone to hold ice cream?

   ____

4. What year will be the 100th anniversary of the 1904 world's fair?

   ____

5. The hot dog was also introduced at the world's fair in 1904. Carla ate her first hot dog in 1987. How many years after the hot dog was introduced did Carla eat her first one?

   ____

6. Approximately 10,984,000 men and approximately 8,927,000 women came to the St. Louis world's fair. How many more men than women visited the fair?

   ____

7. Special buildings were constructed in 1903 to hold displays at the world's fair. How many years old are these buildings now?

   ____

8. The U.S. flag had fewer stars in 1904, but had 13 stripes just as it does today. If 7 of these stripes are red, how many are white?

   ____

USE YOUR CALCULATOR

It is estimated that 450,000 incandescent lights were used at the 1904 world's fair. Thomas Edison perfected the incandescent lamp in 1879. How many years later were so many of them used at the fair?

____

Subtraction

With Renaming

Name ______________________

The Rock Concert

Cindy's older sister took her to see her favorite rock band at the Fox Theater. Read about their evening and answer the questions in complete sentences.

1. How old was Cindy? The concert was in July of 1995. She was born in June of 1984.

   ____

2. They left for the concert at 5:30 P.M. They arrived at 7:30 P.M. How long did it take them to drive?

   ____

3. There were 3,030 seats in the two-level Fox Theater. If 1,275 of the seats were on the ground level, how many were in the balcony?

   ____

4. Earlier that week, her mother had bought Cindy a special outfit to wear to the concert. It cost $43.89. If Mother handed the clerk a $50.00 bill, how much change did she get?

   ____

5. They had a wonderful time. The concert lasted from 8:00 P.M. until 11:30 P.M. How long was the concert?

   ____

6. The feature band played on the stage for 2 hours and 15 minutes. How much of the total concert time did that band <u>not</u> play?

   ____

7. Before the feature band, a "warm-up" band played. How long did the warm-up band play?

   ____

8. Cindy bought a souvenir T-shirt after the concert. Of the 3,020 people who attended the concert, 243 bought T-shirts. How many did not buy a T-shirt?

   ____

9. Cindy also bought a CD for $16.95. If she gave the clerk a $20.00 bill, what was her change?

   ____

USE YOUR CALCULATOR

The odometer on the family car read 39,871 when the two sisters left their driveway at 5:30 that night. It read 40,082 when they got home after the concert. How many total miles did they drive that evening?

____

Addition and Subtraction

Name ______________________________

With Renaming

Halloween Party

When Miguel and Anita planned a Halloween party, they encountered many numbers. Help them solve the equations.

1. The room which they planned to use was 20 feet by 30 feet. What was the perimeter of the room?

   ____

2. If they needed enough crepe paper to go around the perimeter of the room twice, how many feet of crepe paper should they buy?

   ____

3. Miguel bought a box of 50 invitations. They sent an invitation to 25 girls and 23 boys. How many invitations were left over?

   ____

4. They bought a Halloween party kit for $13.50, 5 pumpkins for $2.00 each, and 10 candles for $1.00 each. How much money did they spend on these party supplies?

   ____

5. It took Anita 1 hour and 15 minutes to carve each jack-o'-lantern. How long did she spend carving the five jack-o'-lanterns?

   ____

6. Their friend Carlos bought a ghost costume for $4.50 and a jack-o'-lantern flashlight for $3.25. How much did Carlos spend altogether?

   ____

7. Another friend, Lupita, bought 2 yards of orange cloth at $1.59 per yard and a package of elastic for $.98. Using those materials, her mother made a jack-o'-lantern costume for Lupita and stuffed it with newspaper. How much did her costume cost?

   ____

8. The children bought 108 apples. They made 50 candied apples and used the rest for the game, *Bobbing for Apples*. How many apples did they use for the game?

   ____

9. After the party, Juan won the prize for the best costume. He came as a broom. He wrapped his upper body in black crepe paper and wore a straw skirt around his hips. The crepe paper was $.49 and the straw skirt was $.69. How much did the walking broom spend on his costume?

   ____

USE YOUR CALCULATOR

After the party, 48 guests cleaned up. If each person spent 30 minutes cleaning up, how many combined hours did it take to help clean up?

____

Multiplication and Division

Name ____________________

Flight

The Young Eagle's club made an informational book about airplanes to show their classmates what they were learning. Complete each problem they proposed.

1. Ray read about the first airplane made by the Wright brothers. It reached 30 miles per hour on its first flight. If a small, propeller-driven, single-engine plane flies about 5 times this fast, at what speed can it fly?

   ____

2. Amy's father is a pilot on a jet airliner. He flies from Chicago to Los Angeles, a distance of 2,000 miles. If the jet flew at 500 miles per hour, how long would it take him to fly from Chicago to Los Angeles?

   ____

3. Last summer, Barbara's family flew in a four-engine propeller plane from Chicago to Glacier National Park. It took them 3 hours. If the plane flew 400 miles per hour, how many miles was it from Chicago to Glacier National Park?

   ____

4. The supersonic transport travels 1,500 miles per hour. If it takes 2 hours to fly from New York to London, how many miles is the flight between these cities?

   ____

5. If a twin-engine jet flies about 500 miles an hour, which plane described above travels about 3 times as fast?

   ____

6. Most people choose to fly on the jumbo jet. If it travels at 600 miles per hour, how long would it take to travel the 3,000 miles from New York to London?

   ____

7. How long would it take to fly the 3,000 miles from New York to London in a twin-engine jet if it flies 500 miles per hour?

   ____

8. The Wright brothers' plane could never have flown the 3,000 miles from New York to London, but if it had been possible to fly that far at 30 miles per hour, how long would it have taken?

   ____

USE YOUR CALCULATOR

Lee took a trip with his uncle who flies a small, single-engine, propeller plane. They flew 4 hours from Chicago to Atlanta, then 4 more hours to Miami. If the plane flies 150 miles per hour, how many miles did they fly from Chicago to Miami?

____

Multiplication

Name ____________________

Zoo Information

Mrs. Carson's class gathered information about African animals from the zoo. They came back to school with the following problems. Answer in complete sentences.

1. Each tiger at the zoo eats about 85 pounds of meat in a week. How many pounds of meat must the zoo provide each week for the 14 tigers it owns?

   ____

2. The baby gorilla at the zoo weighed only 5 pounds at birth. Its father weighed 90 times as much. How much did the father gorilla weigh?

   ____

3. If an elephant eats about 95 pounds of food a day, how much food will the elephant eat in a year?

   ____

4. Each hyena eats about 3 pounds of food a day. How many pounds of food will a pack of 15 hyenas need for 31 days?

   ____

5. A hippopotamus requires about 50 pounds of food per day to maintain its weight. How much does it weigh if its weight is about 110 times its daily food intake?

   ____

6. An average lion eats about 75 pounds of meat at a time. It eats about 3 times a week. About how many pounds of meat will it eat in one year?

   ____

7. A large antelope called the eland stands about 6 feet tall. It can stretch its neck and eat from the tops of trees which are 1.5 times taller. How tall are these trees?

   ____

8. A baby elephant may weigh about 250 pounds at birth. By the time it is an adult, it weighs 50 times as much. How much does the adult elephant weigh?

   ____

USE YOUR CALCULATOR

Each ostrich needs a pen about 20 feet by 10 feet. How many square feet of space will be needed by 11 ostriches?

____

Multiplication

Name ______________________

Running a Truck Farm

Mark lives on a farm where he and his family raise fruits and vegetables and ship them to market by truck. Read about the farm and answer the questions in complete sentences.

1. They planted 98 rows of corn with 125 plants in each row. How many corn plants did they plant?

   ____

2. While picking peaches, they filled 742 bushel baskets. Each basket held 45 peaches. How many peaches did they pick?

   ____

3. 41 plums were packed in 1-peck cartons. If there were 237 cartons, how many plums were packed?

   ____

4. The truck made deliveries in a 191-kilometer route each day for 23 days of the busiest month. How many total kilometers did the truck travel in that one month?

   ____

5. The family picked 15 cartons of green beans daily. If each carton held about 300 green beans, about how many green beans did they pick?

   ____

6. When the cantaloupes were ripe, they shipped 430 cases each day. If a case held 12 cantaloupes, how many cantaloupes were shipped each day?

   ____

7. Mark's father works an average of 48 hours a week. If he works 45 weeks of the year, about how many hours does he work in a year?

   ____

8. Mark gets paid $3.00 for each case of corn he picks. If he picked 27 cases of corn last week, how much money did he earn?

   ____

9. Mark's brother John drives the tractor which plants the crops. He gets paid $9.50 per hour. If he worked 48 hours this week, how much would he be paid?

   ____

USE YOUR CALCULATOR

One grocery store that sells this produce serves an average of 349 customers each day. The store is open 364 days a year. About how many people come to the store in a year?

____

$+¢−x÷=$+¢−x÷=$+¢−x÷=$+¢−x÷=$

Mixed Operations

Name ______________________________

Add, Subtract, Multiply

The Fishing Trip

Emily and her family take a fishing trip in the mountains each year. Read about their preparations and circle whether to **add**, to **subtract**, or to **multiply**. Write the numerical answer on the correct line.

1. The family bought a large tent for $79.95. They also purchased an ice chest for $11.89. They bought two fuel tanks for the cook stove at $5.00 each. What did they spend altogether for these camping supplies?

   Add _______ **Subtract** _______ **Multiply** _______

2. The three children had outgrown their hiking boots. Boots were on sale for $24.50 each. How much did the three pairs of hiking boots cost?

   Add _______ **Subtract** _______ **Multiply** _______

3. Last year, the food for the 10-day trip cost $259.82. This year, they spent only $186.89 on food. How much less did they spend this year?

   Add _______ **Subtract** _______ **Multiply** _______

4. Each of their six water bottles holds 8 gallons. How many gallons of water did they take?

   Add _______ **Subtract** _______ **Multiply** _______

5. Emily bought 6 new fishing lures. They were $.59, $.89, $.79, $.39, $.69, and $.65. How much did she pay in total for the lures?

   Add _______ **Subtract** _______ **Multiply** _______

6. Emily's mother bought two bottles of sunscreen for $2.39 each, and two bottles of insect spray for $1.29 each. How much did she spend on protection from sun and insects?

   Add _______ **Subtract** _______ **Multiply** _______

7. The fee for camping at the campsite was $6.50 per day. If the family camped there for 10 days, how much did they pay to camp?

   Add _______ **Subtract** _______ **Multiply** _______

USE YOUR CALCULATOR

The altitude at their home was 3,850 feet. The altitude at their campsite was 9,875 feet. How much higher was the altitude at the campsite than at their home?

Add _______ **Subtract** _______ **Multiply** _______

Division

Name ______________________

Service Station Employee

Samantha's big brother, Bert, works at a service station. Read about his job and write each answer in a complete sentence.

1. The service station has a supply of 95 tires. How many sets of 4 tires can be sold from this supply?

   ____

2. If 4 tires cost $259, how much does one tire cost?

   ____

3. The service station made $207.00 changing oil in one day. If they changed the oil for 9 cars, how much did each oil change cost?

   ____

4. Samantha's father filled up his car with $9.81 of gasoline. If he got 9 gallons of gasoline, how much did gas cost per gallon?

   ____

5. Bert counted the service station's supply of spark plugs. Each car takes 4 spark plugs, and he counted 84 spark plugs. How many cars can they service with spark plugs before they need to reorder?

   ____

6. The service station made $315 one week on car washes. If each car wash cost $7, how many cars were washed that week?

   ____

7. Bert makes $35 per day for working at the service station. If he gets paid $5 per hour, how many hours does he work in a day?

   ____

8. During the summer, when Bert isn't in school, he makes $700 a month. If he is paid $35 per day, how many days per month does he work in the summer?

   ____

9. Bert wants to buy a car that costs $2,000. How many days will he have to work to buy the car he wants?

   ____

USE YOUR CALCULATOR

During the school year, Bert makes $35 on Saturdays. He estimated the expenses for his new car will be about $1,400 for a year. How many Saturdays will he have to work to cover the expenses for his car?

____

Division

Name ____________________

Preparing for the Prom

Wayne helped his sister who was on the prom preparation committee. She had these problems to solve. Write the answers in complete sentences.

1. The committee hired a band for the dance for $500. If the dance lasts from 8 P.M. until 12 P.M., how much will the band be paid per hour?

   ____

2. The dance band has 5 members. How much does each band member get paid per hour?

   ____

3. The committee rented 4 special-effects lights for $100. How much would it cost to rent one light?

   ____

4. The committee will rent 256 chairs for the dance. If 4 chairs fit around one table, how many tables will they need to rent?

   ____

5. There is a fountain in the middle of the dance floor that holds 150 gallons of water. The committee has a 5-gallon bucket. How many buckets of water will it take to fill the fountain?

   ____

6. The committee has ordered 192 flowers to be put in vases on the tables. If 3 flowers go in each vase, how many vases will they need?

   ____

7. Wayne helped his sister put crepe paper around the walls of the room. Each wall was 20 yards long. They used 40 yards of crepe paper per wall. Will 160 yards of crepe paper be enough to decorate the square room?

   ____

8. After the prom was over, a cleanup crew of 7 people worked a total of 21 hours to get the room back to order. How many hours did they each work?

   ____

USE YOUR CALCULATOR

The expenses for the prom were $500 for the band, $100 for the lights, $100 for the fountain, $300 for the flowers and vases, and $125 for the crepe paper. If 250 people bought tickets for $5 each, will the prom committee have enough money to cover their expenses?

____

Division

Name ____________________

Miles per Hour

Mrs. Craig brought some posters to her class from a travel agency. She asked her class to make division problems about travel. Read the problems they wrote and write the answers in complete sentences.

1. If a car traveled at an average speed of 55 miles per hour, how long would it take to go 467.5 miles?

   ____

2. A cruise liner traveled 2,520 miles to reach port in 72 hours. How many miles per hour did the cruise ship travel?

   ____

3. A jumbo jet traveled 2,400 miles from Chicago to Mexico in 4 hours. How many miles per hour was it flying?

   ____

4. An express train averaged 70 miles per hour. About how long did it take this train to travel from Chicago to Kansas City, a distance of 665 miles?

   ____

5. If the express train traveled 777 miles from Kansas City to Albuquerque at 70 miles per hour, how many hours would it take to get to Albuquerque?

   ____

6. The distance from Chicago to San Diego is about 2,500 miles. If you wanted to plan an 8-day trip one way, how many miles would you have to drive each day?

   ____

7. If the moon were about 236,952 miles from Earth, and a rocket ship could take you there in 72 hours, how many miles per hour would you be averaging?

   ____

USE YOUR CALCULATOR

The Pony Express ran from St. Joseph, MO, to Sacramento, CA. The riders took 10 days to cover 1,966 miles. If they rode 196.6 miles per day (riding 24 hours a day), how many miles per hour did the Pony Express riders average?

____

Finding Averages

Name ______________________________

Class Averages

Mrs. Corrigan helped her students figure their average score on the tests they took. Read about the various scores and write a complete answer.

1. Out of 100 points possible on the first math test, the total for 24 students was 2,064 points. What was the class average? Emily made 94 points on the test. Was Emily above or below average?

   ____

2. If Bob made 58 points on the same test, was he above or below average?

   ____

3. On the second math test, the total for 23 students was 2,047 points. Ken was not present for the test. When he made it up, above what number did he have to score to be above average?

   ____

4. On the third test, the total for 24 students was 1,824 points. If Darnell's score was 82, did he make a score above or below average?

   ____

5. Mrs. Corrigan provided her class with some more practice on division with 2-digit divisors, and she gave them the third test again. This time their total points equaled 2,040 for 24 students. What was their average this time? By how much did their average improve?

   ____

6. She threw out the lowest score for each student, and averaged the three remaining scores. The test averages were 86, 89, and 85. What is the overall average for the first quarter grade?

   ____

7. The science tests were averaged the same way. Ms. Molecule totaled 2,184 points for her 24 students on the first test. If Bill had a score of 87, was he above or below average?

   ____

8. On the second science test, the 24 students earned a total of 2,232 points. What was the class average for test two?

   ____

9. On the third science test, 24 students earned a total of 2,140 points. What was the average score? Do you think the students were more prepared for this science test than for the third math test?

   ____

USE YOUR CALCULATOR

Anyone in the class with a 92 average or better got an *A*. Yakira had scores in Math of 91, 93 and 97. Did Yakira get an *A*?

____

Mixed Operations

Name ______________________________

Add, Subtract, Multiply, and Divide

Skate-A-Thon

The fifth grade of Honeywell School sponsored a Skate-A-Thon to help raise money for a local children's hospital. Read each problem. Circle whether to **add**, **subtract**, **multiply**, or **divide**. Write the answer to the question on the correct line.

1. Gregory's father was the director for the Skate-A-Thon. He required that each child bring their own skates and safety helmets. 37 of 42 students who entered the event already had skates, and 20 had a helmet. How many students needed to buy or rent skates and helmets?

   Add _______ **Subtract** _______ **Multiply** _______ **Divide** _______

2. Marianne saved $10 a week from baby-sitting to pay for new skates and a helmet. She paid $45 for skates and $25 for a helmet. How many weeks did she have to save $10?

   Add _______ **Subtract** _______ **Multiply** _______ **Divide** _______

3. Elizabeth decided her skate wheels were worn out. She paid $19.90 for a new set. How much change did she get back from a $20.00 bill?

   Add _______ **Subtract** _______ **Multiply** _______ **Divide** _______

4. For five days, the students practiced in a local roller rink to get in shape for the Skate-A-Thon. It cost each child $1.75 per day to get into the rink. How much did 42 students pay in all?

   Add _______ **Subtract** _______ **Multiply** _______ **Divide** _______

5. The students asked people to pledge $.50 for every mile they skated. If Orlando skated 16 miles, how much money would he collect?

   Add _______ **Subtract** _______ **Multiply** _______ **Divide** _______

6. The park in which they held the Skate-A-Thon had one 4-mile paved trail and one 8-mile paved trail. What route might a student take who wanted to skate 12 miles? List different possibilities.

   ____

USE YOUR CALCULATOR

If each student skated an average of 14 miles, how many miles did 42 students skate?

____

How much money did they raise for the hospital at $.50 per mile?

____

Decimals

Addition and Subtraction

Name ______________________

Vitamin C

For her science fair project, Maggie wanted to see if taking vitamin C helped ward off colds. She asked her friends to help her by keeping track of the amount of vitamin C they took each day. Each friend was supposed to take in at least 60 percent of the recommended daily allowance (RDA) of vitamin C for breakfast. Write each answer in a complete sentence.

1. Lynn drank 1 glass of orange juice containing 100% RDA vitamin C, and 1 cup of milk containing 1.84% of vitamin C, and ate 1 cup of corn flakes containing 25.8% RDA of vitamin C. Did she take 60% of the RDA of vitamin C? How much was she over or under her goal?

   ____

2. Wesley ate a 1/2 cup of strawberries containing 74.46% RDA of vitamin C, 1 egg containing 0 vitamin C, and 1 piece of toast containing 0 vitamin C. Did he reach his goal of 60% RDA of vitamin C? How much was he under or over his goal?

   ____

3. Emily ate 1 cup of raisin flake cereal with 0% RDA of vitamin C, and 1 cup of milk with 1.84% RDA of vitamin C. Did she reach her goal? If she had added 1 glass of orange juice at 100% RDA, how much vitamin C would she have had that day?

   ____

4. Sarah ate 1/2 grapefruit at 62.50% RDA, a piece of toast at 0% RDA and hot chocolate at 2.52% RDA of vitamin C. How much was she under or over her goal?

   ____

5. Brian ate 1/2 cup of strawberries with 74.46% RDA of vitamin C, 1 cup of milk with 1.84% RDA of vitamin C, and 1 cup of raisin flakes cereal with 0 vitamin C. Did he reach his goal? How much was he under or over the goal?

   ____

6. Which student had the most vitamin C for breakfast?

   ____

7. Which kind of foods seemed to have the most vitamin C?

   ____

EXTENSION

Did you have 60% or more of the RDA of vitamin C for breakfast today? Use nutritional information on packages or from a cookbook to calculate.

____

Decimals

Money

Name ____________________

Shopping for Gifts

A group of friends went to the mall to look for gifts for their family and friends at the holiday season. Read about their choices and write complete answers.

1. Heather looked for a pair of silver earrings for her sister. One pair was $19.95, and the other pair was $12.49. How much less did the second pair cost?

   ____

2. Fred chose a mug for his teacher which cost $4.79. How much change did he get from a $10 bill?

   ____

3. Since Lani loved music boxes, she bought one for each of her two sisters. One music box cost $18.59, and the other was $16.99. How much did she spend on music boxes?

   ____

4. Peggy bought some piano sheet music for the holidays. The first piece was $3.39, the second was $2.95, and the third was $4.49. How much did she pay for the three pieces of sheet music?

   ____

5. Bill only brought $20.00 with him. He bought a shirt for his dad for $14.79. Then, he found a sweater for his mother which was on sale for only $9.88. How much would he have to borrow from John to buy the sweater?

   ____

6. Barry had 3 ten-dollar bills. He wanted to buy his brother a football for $9.95 and a soccer ball for his sister which cost $14.49. Does he have enough money? How much more does he need, or how much change will he get?

   ____

7. While they were shopping, Peggy and Lani stopped for lunch. They each bought a soda at $1.19 each, and they split a hamburger which was $1.49. How much was their lunch bill?

   ____

8. Rachel bought a charm for her mother's bracelet. It cost $8.99. Last year she spent only $5.59 on a charm. How much more did the charm cost her this year?

   ____

USE YOUR CALCULATOR

Rachel's mother gave the children a ride to the mall. When they left home to pick up the children, the car's odometer read 85,661.5. After she took each one back home, the odometer read 85,693.9. How many miles had she driven?

____

Decimals

Thousandths Place

Name ______________________

Batting Averages

In baseball, the batting averages are expressed in decimals to the thousandths place. A batting average is the number of hits divided by the number of times a player has been at bat. List these great hitters in order of their batting averages, from most to least. Then answer the questions below.

Ty Cobb	0.367	Rogers Hornsby	0.358
Babe Ruth	0.342	Lou Gehrig	0.340
Joe DiMaggio	0.325	Ted Williams	0.406

____

____

____

____

____

____

1. How much higher was the average of the man in first place than the man in second place?

____

2. How much lower was the batting average of the man in last place than the man in second place?

____

3. Jackie Robinson had a batting average of 0.342. How much lower was his batting average than Ted Williams's?

____

4. Willie Mays had a batting average of 0.302. How much lower was his than Babe Ruth's average?

____

5. The pitcher for the Eagles had an earned run average of 3.56 last year. The pitcher for the Blue Jays had an average of 4.37. Which pitcher had the greater earned run average? How much greater was it?

____

USE YOUR CALCULATOR

If a team had a winning record of 0.647 one year, 0.740 the next year, and 0.635 the third year, what was their average winning record for the three years?

____

If they excluded the score of the second year, and averaged only the first and third years, what would their average winning record have been?

____

Decimals

Multiplication

Name ____________________

Bicycle Data

Dana had a three-speed bicycle. She noticed that the bike wheel went around fewer times in first gear with one turn of the pedals than with one turn in third gear. She read in her bike manual that the gear ratio for third gear was 3.7, for second gear 2.5, and for first gear 1.4. The gear ratio is the number of turns of the wheel compared to the number of turns of the gear, or pedals. Multiply the circumference of her bike wheel by the ratio of the gear to find the distance traveled by her bike.

1. The circumference of Dana's wheel is 1.95 meters. She measured on the pavement to find out exactly how far the wheel had traveled in two turns of the pedals in third gear (ratio of 3.7). How many meters did it go?

   ____

2. Dana then measured to find out exactly how far the wheel had traveled in two turns of the pedals in second gear (ratio of 2.5). How many meters did it go this time?

   ____

3. Finally, she measured the distance her bike traveled in two turns of the pedals in first gear (ratio of 1.4). How many meters did the wheel go in first gear?

   ____

4. How much farther did the bicycle go in third gear for two turns of the pedals than in first gear for two turns?

   ____

5. Dana measured the distance her bike traveled in third gear for 25 turns of the pedals. How many meters did the bike go?

   ____

Answer the following.

6. Dana and her next-door neighbor, Kathryn, rode their bikes 4.1 kilometers to a friend's pool to swim. How far did each go both ways?

   ____

7. If they went swimming 6 days in the week, how many kilometers would each ride in a week?

   ____

8. Will they have to turn their pedals more often if they are using first gear or third gear?

   ____

USE YOUR CALCULATOR

Dana rode her bike to Kathryn's house for 2 pedal turns in first gear, then 2 turns in second gear, and 2 turns in third gear. How many meters is it to Kathryn's door?

____

Decimals

Multiplication

Name ______________________________

Delivering Encyclopedias

Scott's big brother, Leon, works as a delivery person for an encyclopedia company. Answer each question below about his work.

1. A small box of books weighs 8.3 pounds. A large box weighs 3 times as much. How much does the large box weigh?

   ____

2. When someone buys a set of encyclopedias, the books come in 7 large boxes and 3 small boxes. How much does the whole set weigh?

   ____

3. In five days last week, Leon drove an average of 46.5 miles each day. How many total miles did he drive last week?

   ____

4. Leon uses his own van to make deliveries, and the company pays him $.30 a mile to cover expenses. How much money was paid to Leon for his travel expenses last week?

   ____

5. The five grade schools in Scottsdale each ordered a new set of the encyclopedias. Using the weight from problem 2, calculate how many pounds of encyclopedias Leon delivered to the school warehouse.

   ____

6. The company awarded five unabridged dictionaries as a free bonus for ordering 5 sets of the encyclopedias. Each dictionary weighed 5.48 pounds. How much weight did the 5 dictionaries add to the delivery?

   ____

7. On days when he is not making deliveries, Leon works in the warehouse getting orders ready to ship out of town. One day he boxed 27 sets of encyclopedias. Using the weight from problem two, how much did the 27 sets weigh?

   ____

8. Leon took the 27 sets of encyclopedias to the shipper. He divided the load evenly for 3 trips. How many pounds did he carry in each trip? How many sets did he take in each trip?

   ____

USE YOUR CALCULATOR

Leon makes $8.64 an hour for his delivery and packaging work. If he works 40 hours a week, what are his wages for the week?

____

Decimals

Mixed Operations

Name ____________________

Physical Fitness

The P. E. teacher at Marcy School was helping the children get in shape for the national fitness test. Read each problem and circle whether to **add**, **subtract** or **multiply**. Write the answer on the correct line.

1. Janet jogged 1 mile on Monday, 2.6 miles on Tuesday, 1.5 miles on Wednesday, 2.25 miles on Thursday, and 4.1 miles on Friday. How many miles did she jog this week?

   Add ______ **Subtract** ______ **Multiply** ______

2. Bart did 75 sit-ups every school day this week. How many sit-ups did he do this week?

   Add ______ **Subtract** ______ **Multiply** ______

3. Randy did .48 as many sit-ups as Bart. How many sit-ups did Randy do this week?

   Add ______ **Subtract** ______ **Multiply** ______

4. Marilyn can do 35 chin-ups without stopping. The next best person in the class can chin .60 as many times as Marilyn can. How many chin-ups can he do?

   Add ______ **Subtract** ______ **Multiply** ______

5. Ebony can run the mile in 9.75 minutes. Crystal runs the mile in 8.6 minutes. In how many fewer minutes can Crystal run the mile?

   Add ______ **Subtract** ______ **Multiply** ______

6. Thomas is 5 feet 3 inches tall. The recommended weight for boys this height is 123.5. If Thomas weighs 126.8, how much weight should he lose before taking the national fitness test?

   Add ______ **Subtract** ______ **Multiply** ______

7. Deana jumps the rope an average of 85.6 times without stopping. Terri's average is 3.2 times Deana's average. What is Terri's average for jumping rope?

   Add ______ **Subtract** ______ **Multiply** ______

USE YOUR CALCULATOR

On the day of the fitness test, 156 students took the test. If .75 of them passed all the tests, how many students is that?

Add ______ **Subtract** ______ **Multiply** ______

Fractions

Concepts

Name ______________________

Story Problems

Ms. Jeffrey's class wrote math problems that use fractions. Solve these problems.

1. A Clydesdale horse could weigh 1/2 a ton. If a camel weighed 900 pounds, which animal would weigh more?

   ____

2. It took Jeremy 20 minutes to do the dishes. His sister can do them in 1/4 of an hour. Who can do the dishes in less time?

   ____

3. A prize-winning tomato weighs 480 grams. A big, red onion weighs 4/10 of a kilogram. Which weighs more, the tomato or the onion?

   ____

4. Ian ate 1/4 of the pizza. Cory ate 1/5 of the pizza. Phillip ate 1/2 of the pizza. Who ate the most pizza?

   ____

5. Lupe's hamburger weighed 5/16 of a pound. Was it smaller or larger than a quarter-pound hamburger?

   ____

6. Eric's shoe is 8 inches long. His brother Bobby's shoe measures 1/2 of a foot long. Which boy is probably older? Explain.

   ____

7. Their father's shoe measures 13 inches. Is their father's shoe longer or shorter than 1/3 of a yard?

   ____

8. Jane measured 3/4 of a cup of milk. If her recipe called for 5/8 of a cup, should she add milk or pour some of it out of the cup?

   ____

9. Jackie took 13 minutes to braid her hair. Her mother takes 1/6 of an hour to comb her own hair. Which takes longer, Jackie's hair or her mother's hair?

   ____

10. Patty and Charles are reading the same 250-page book. Patty has read 1/2 of the book. Charles is on page 189. Who has read more of the book?

    ____

USE YOUR CALCULATOR

Evelyn's dad owns an orchard with four kinds of fruit trees. 1/5 of the orchard is in pear trees. 5/100 of the orchard is in apricot trees. 1/2 of the orchard is in apple trees. The rest of the orchard is in peach trees. How much of the orchard is in peach trees? ______________

Fractions

Name ____________________

Conversion

Calculate the number of units in each fraction described.

1. If there are 12 eggs in a dozen, how many eggs are in...
   - 1/2 dozen? ____________
   - 1/4 dozen? ____________
   - 1/3 dozen? ____________
2. If there are 100 centimeters (cm) in a meter, how many cm are in...
   - 1/2 meter? ____________
   - 1/4 meter? ____________
   - 1/10 meter? ____________
3. If there are 16 ounces in a pound, how many ounces are in...
   - 1/2 pound? ____________
   - 1/4 pound? ____________
   - 3/8 pound? ____________
4. If there are 4 quarts in a gallon, how many quarts are in...
   - 1/2 of a gallon? ____________
   - 1/4 of a gallon? ____________
   - 3/4 of a gallon? ____________
5. If there are 60 seconds in a minute, how many seconds are in...
   - 1/2 of a minute? ____________
   - 1/4 of a minute? ____________
   - 3/4 of a minute? ____________
6. If there are 1,000 meters in a kilometer, how many meters are there in...
   - 1/10 of a kilometer? ____________
   - 1/2 of a kilometer? ____________
   - 1/4 of a kilometer? ____________
7. If there are 30 days in most months, how many days are there in...
   - 1/3 of a month? ____________
   - 1/6 of a month? ____________
   - 1/10 of a month? ____________
8. If there are 24 hours in one day, how many hours are there in...
   - 1/3 of a day? ____________
   - 2/3 of a day? ____________
   - 1/4 of a day? ____________
9. If there are 36 inches in one yard, how many inches are there in...
   - 2/3 of a yard? ____________
   - 1/4 of a yard? ____________
   - 1/2 of a yard? ____________
10. If there are 2,000 pounds in one ton, how many pounds are there in...
    - 1/2 of a ton? ____________
    - 1/4 of a ton? ____________
    - 1/20 of a ton? ____________

USE YOUR CALCULATOR

If there are 5,280 feet in one mile, how many feet are there in...

- 1/2 of a mile? ____________
- 2/5 of a mile? ____________
- 3/4 of a mile? ____________

Fractions

Concepts

Name ____________________

Reduce It

Reduce each fraction in the sentences below to its lowest terms. Rewrite the sentence correctly on the line.

1. Daniel slept 8/24 of a day.

   ____

2. Emilia rides the bus to school 6/8 of the time.

   ____

3. Jim spent 5/25 of his dollar at the candy store.

   ____

4. Josie completed 80/100 of her math problems correctly.

   ____

5. Amy scored 4/8 of the points in the soccer game.

   ____

6. The sun was hidden by clouds 20/30 of the days in January.

   ____

7. The cars raced 20/60 of the hour.

   ____

8. The baby cried for 10/60 of an hour.

   ____

9. Of the students in Maureen's room, 8/24 have pets.

   ____

10. Ethan drank 6/12 of the sodas in one day.

    ____

11. Of the students in the band, 4/16 played saxophone.

    ____

12. 9/27 of the vehicles are trucks.

    ____

13. In the lunchroom, a child drank 250/1000 liter of milk.

    ____

14. 18/20 of the class will be in the holiday program.

    ____

USE YOUR CALCULATOR

The space shuttle was 8/1028 of its way to the planet Mars.

____

Fractions

Name ________________________

A Trip to the Ocean

Maria's girls' club earned enough money from their cookie sale to have a camp out at the ocean. Read about their trip and write your answers in complete sentences.

1. The bus started with 6 1/2 gallons of gasoline. When the driver added 9 1/2 more gallons of gasoline, how much gasoline did the bus have in it?

   ____

2. The girls and their leaders stopped for a picnic after driving 58 1/5 miles. After the picnic, they drove 43 4/5 miles before reaching the ocean. How far were they from home?

   ____

3. Before leaving home, they had made sandwiches for their lunch. They had 7 1/2 tuna sandwiches, 4 1/4 cheese sandwiches, 2 3/4 peanut butter sandwiches, and 5 1/2 beef sandwiches. How many total sandwiches did they bring?

   ____

4. The leader cut their watermelon into 16 slices for lunch. They ate 8 of the slices. What fraction of the watermelon did they eat?

   ____

5. If they saved the rest of the watermelon for dinner, how much was left for their dinner?

   ____

6. When they arrived, they took 1 1/3 hours to set up the tents. They spent another 2/3 hour getting their bedrolls ready. How long did they work before they could play in the ocean?

   ____

7. The girls swam and played in the water for 1 3/4 hours. Then they sat in the sun for 3/4 hour. How many hours did they play and sunbathe?

   ____

8. After dinner, they had a campfire. First, they sang for 1 1/3 hours. Then, they told ghost stories for 2/3 hour. If they put out the fire and went to sleep at 10:30, what time did they begin the campfire?

   ____

9. The next morning, 3/8 of the girls went fishing. The rest of the girls hunted for shells. If there were 8 girls altogether, how many hunted for shells? How many went fishing?

   ____

USE YOUR CALCULATOR

The bus used 28 gallons of gasoline. If gasoline cost $1.19 per gallon, how much did they spend in all on gasoline?

____

If that was 1/2 of the money they spent on the trip, how much did they spend in all?

____

Fractions

Name ______________________

Cooking for a Crowd

Amy and Gina helped their mother and father prepare the food for the party after their new baby brother's christening. Read about their day and answer the questions in complete sentences.

1. The recipe for crab dip calls for 3/4 cup of sour cream. Amy has a 3-cup container of sour cream. Does she have enough sour cream to triple the recipe?

   ____

2. For the apple salad, they have cut up 6 1/3 cups of apples, 2 2/3 cups of celery, and 2/3 cup of nuts. How many cups must the salad bowl be able to hold?

   ____

3. The girls put 1/5 of the grapes on a platter and 2/5 of the grapes in a basket. They put the rest in the refrigerator. What fraction of the grapes are in the refrigerator?

   ____

4. Gina put 32 slices of bread on the table. 1/2 of the bread is wheat bread and 1/2 is rye bread. How many slices are wheat bread?

   ____

5. Gina put 3/4 cup of mayonnaise into a bowl. Later in the party, she added 1/4 cup more mayonnaise. How much mayonnaise did she put out?

   ____

6. The girls put out 3 1/2 pounds of potato chips and 3 3/4 pounds of corn chips on the tables. How many pounds of chips did they put out?

   ____

7. Mother made 8 1/3 quarts of lemonade and 9 5/6 quarts of tea for the guests. How many quarts of drinks did she prepare?

   ____

8. Their father bought a sheet cake decorated with the baby's name and the date. They cut it into 28 pieces. After the party, 4 pieces were left. What fraction of the cake was left?

   ____

9. The baby received 14 gifts at the party. If Mother wrote 1/2 of the thank-you notes the next day, how many thank-you notes did she have left to write?

   ____

USE YOUR CALCULATOR

They used 3 1/2 bags of ice at the party. If each bag holds 100 cubes of ice, how many cubes of ice did they use?

____

Fractions

Name ______________________

Love That Motorcycle

James loved to ride on his uncle's motorcycle. Read about his adventures and write the answers in complete sentences.

1. James and his uncle rode 9 3/4 total miles on flat and hilly country. 2 1/4 miles of their ride was on flat roads. How many miles did they ride in the hilly country?

   ____

2. Last week, his uncle took him to a spring festival in another town. When they began, the motorcycle's tank was full with 5 gallons of gasoline. When they got back, his uncle put in 2 3/4 gallons to fill it up. How many gallons did they not use?

   ____

3. The new helmet James's uncle bought for himself cost $54. He bought one for James for 1/2 as much. How much did the helmet for James cost?

   ____

4. His uncle gave him a ride to school one day. It is 4 1/10 miles from James's house to school. They passed Harold's house after 2 2/10 miles. How far is it from Harold's house to school?

   ____

5. The motorcycle usually holds 3 quarts of oil. One day, it developed a leak and only 3/4 quart of oil was left. How much oil had leaked out?

   ____

6. James and his uncle went on a long trip to see James's grandmother. They stopped for breakfast when they had gone 1/5 of the way. They stopped for lunch when they had gone another 2/5 of the way. How much of the trip did they have yet to complete?

   ____

7. James noticed that each 1/5 of the trip took them 1 hour. How many hours had they been traveling when they stopped for lunch?

   ____

8. How many total hours would it take them to drive straight to Grandmother's house?

   ____

USE YOUR CALCULATOR

James's uncle makes payments on the motorcycle. So far, he has paid for 1/4 of the motorcycle in 1 year. How many more years will he be making payments on the motorcycle?

____

Fractions

Name ________________________

Pleasure Boating

Gerald's dad has a boat store near a large lake. Read about the problems Gerald encounters. Write the answers in complete sentences.

1. Gerald's favorite boat at the store is 22 2/4 feet long. Another boat they sell is 5 1/4 feet shorter. How long is the second boat?

   ____

2. Gerald's dad usually spends about 1/2 of his working time in the store and 1/2 of his time in boats on the lake with customers. If Dad works 40 hours a week, about how much time a week does he spend in the store?

   ____

3. Gerald and his dad took their boat out on Saturday for 3 hours. They spent 2 1/4 hours fishing. They rode around for a while before they went home. How long did they ride around?

   ____

4. The anchor on the boat has 300 total feet of rope. 100 feet of the rope is cotton, and the rest is a special sturdy nylon rope. What fraction of the rope is nylon?

   ____

5. The boat had 15 2/3 gallons of gasoline in it. When full, it holds 30 2/3 gallons. How much gasoline would fill it up?

   ____

6. Gerald has a rope which is 8 3/4 feet long. He used 6 1/4 feet to tie the boat to the dock. How much rope did he have left to coil neatly on the dock?

   ____

7. Every spring, Gerald and his dad scraped the barnacles off the boat. It took them 8 3/4 hours this year. Last year it only took them 3 1/4 hours. How much longer did it take them this year?

   ____

8. Sometimes they put the boat on a trailer and took it to another lake. It takes them 3 1/4 hours to get there. Once they had a flat tire after they had driven 1 1/4 hours. How many hours were they from the other lake?

   ____

9. Their trip took them 4 3/4 hours. Since it usually takes 3 1/4 hours to get there, how long must it have taken them to change the tire?

   ____

USE YOUR CALCULATOR

Gerald plans to buy a boat when he is 20 years old. He thinks he will have lived 1/4 of his life by then. To what age does Gerald think he will live?

____

Fractions

Mixed Operations

Name ______________________

Paint, Plaster, and Other Problems

Patricia's mother runs a home-decorating store. She helped Patricia write these fraction problems. Can you solve them?

1. Alice spent two days painting her bedroom. She painted 1 1/3 hours on Wednesday and 2 1/3 hours on Thursday. How many hours did she paint in all?

 ____

2. Mr. Lennett painted 3 rooms in his house. It took him 2 2/3 hours to paint the first room. The second room took 2 1/3 hours, and the third room took 2 hours. How long did it take him to paint 3 rooms?

 ____

3. Mr. Riley purchased 2 gallons of paint. If the hall took 1 1/4 gallons of paint, how much paint did he have left?

 ____

4. Patricia's mother had just tiled a kitchen floor. She put down 23 1/2 tiles on one side of the sink, and 37 3/4 tiles on the other side. How many tiles did she lay in all?

 ____

5. Carpet was on sale. On the first day, one roll of carpet started with 100 yards on it. They sold 29 3/4 yards in the morning and 32 1/8 yards in the afternoon. How much carpet was left from their 100-yard roll?

 ____

6. Mrs. Kester plans to wallpaper her kitchen and bathroom. The kitchen will take 56 2/3 square feet of wallpaper. The bathroom will take 31 1/3 square feet of wallpaper. How many feet of wallpaper should Mrs. Kester buy?

 ____

7. Mrs. Kester will need 1 1/4 bags of wallpaper paste for the bathroom and 2 3/4 bags for the kitchen. How many bags should Mrs. Kester buy?

 ____

8. Mrs. Kester bought material for new drapes. She bought 27 1/2 yards for the living room curtains. She needed 14 1/4 fewer yards for the dining room curtains. How many yards did she need for the dining room?

 ____

USE YOUR CALCULATOR

Patricia helped her mother with the tile job. She was paid $25 for her work. She made 1/4 what her mother was paid. How much was her mother paid?

____

Fractions

Mixed Operations

Name ____________________

State Trivia Game

When Mrs. Campbell's class studied about their state, they wrote questions about the state involving fractions for a game. Answer their questions in complete sentences.

1. In 1850, there were about 6 1/2 million pine trees in our state. Most of the pine trees were cut down for lumber early in this century. Now about 1 1/3 million pine trees exist in the state. About how many pine trees were lost?

   ____

2. Our state has two major cities. City A has 4 1/2 million people. City B has 3 1/6 million people. How many more people does city A have than city B?

   ____

3. Many of the people in our state work in auto manufacturing. Company A employs 1/2 as many people as company B. If company B employs 50,000 people, how many people does company A employ?

   ____

4. The students in Mrs. Campbell's class decided that 1/4 of the time it is too hot in their state, and 1/4 of the time it is too cold. How much of the time is the temperature just right?

   ____

5. Our state has many rivers and parks. About 1 4/12 million people go camping each year. About 9/12 million people go canoeing each year. How many more people camp than canoe?

   ____

6. Of all the cities in the state, about 1/3 of them have a population under 25,000. What fraction has a population over 25,000?

   ____

7. During the Ice Age, a glacier covered about 3/5 of our state. About how much of the state was not covered by a glacier?

   ____

8. A major river is about 2,400 miles long in total. About 1/6 of the river runs through our state. How many miles of the river run through our state?

   ____

USE YOUR CALCULATOR

Our school has about 450 students. Our students represent about 1/1000 of the elementary school students in the state. About how many elementary school students are in our state?

____

Fractions

Multiplication

Name ____________________

Stump the Teacher

The students in Mr. Davidson's class were playing "stump the teacher." See if you can solve their problems.

1. If baseball cards are worth 1/10 of a dollar each, how much are Brad's 54 cards worth?

   ____

2. If 6/8 of Sally's 8 puppies are female and 1/2 of the female puppies have been sold, how many female puppies have been sold?

   ____

3. Felipe used 2/3 cup of cheese for each pizza. If he made 4 pizzas, how much cheese did he need to buy?

   ____

4. There was 3/4 of a cherry pie in the refrigerator. If Sue ate 1/3 of that, how much of the total pie did she eat?

   ____

5. Francis bought 15/16 of a yard of fabric. She used 1/2 of it to make a dress for her doll. What fraction of a yard did she use?

   ____

6. If a lot is 5/8 of an acre, and the house covers 1/2 of it, what fraction of an acre is covered by the house?

   ____

7. At the track fair, I entered 5 sprint contests. If each race was 1/4 mile long, how many miles did I sprint in all?

   ____

8. The class had 1/4 of an hour to take a math quiz. Nate used only 1/3 of the time. What fraction of an hour did Nate use for the quiz?

   ____

9. Sally and Kim live 3/8 of a mile apart. If they each walked 1/2 of the way and met in the middle, what part of a mile did each walk?

   ____

10. This year's summer vacation was 1/6 of the year. How many months long was the summer vacation this year?

    ____

11. Paul's dog was asleep 2/3 of the day. How many hours was it awake?

    ____

12. The principal divided a bulletin board into thirds. He used 1/3 of 2/3 of the bulletin board for bus schedules. How much of the total bulletin board was used for bus schedules?

    ____

13. The art teacher gave Saul 1/2 of a bottle of glue. He used 3/4 of the glue. What part of the whole bottle of glue was left when he was done?

    ____

Fractions

Multiplying Mixed Numbers

Name ______________________

Cooking Conversions

Beth and her mother were cooking a birthday dinner for Beth's father. They were serving fresh pasta with chicken and mushrooms for ten people. The recipe served only four people. They multiplied each ingredient by 2 1/2 to get the correct amount. Read each recipe ingredient and write the amount they will use on the line.

1. 1/4 pound of butter ______________________
2. 1/3 cup of flour ______________________
3. 2 1/2 cups chicken stock ______________________
4. 3/4 cup cream ______________________
5. 1/4 cup wine ______________________
6. 2 teaspoons salt ______________________
7. 1/4 teaspoon pepper ______________________
8. 1 cup sliced mushrooms ______________________
9. 6 mushroom caps ______________________
10. 1 cup cooked ham ______________________
11. 1/2 pound pasta dough ______________________
12. 2 cups cooked chicken ______________________
13. 1/3 cup grated cheese ______________________

For dessert, they made an apple tart. Convert the recipe for four people to amounts for ten people.

1. 1/2 pound butter ______________________
2. 1 cup brown sugar ______________________
3. 3 cups apple slices ______________________
4. 1/4 cup almonds ______________________
5. 2 teaspoons lemon juice ______________________
6. 1/4 teaspoon cinnamon ______________________
7. 1 1/4 cups flour ______________________
8. 1 teaspoon sugar ______________________
9. 2 eggs ______________________

Measurement

Metric Length

Name ______________________________

How Far? How Long?

Ms. Martinez made this sign about metric length for her class. Refer to the sign to answer the questions below.

1 kilometer = 1000 meters 1 meter = 100 centimeters 1 centimeter = 10 millimeters	km = kilometer m = meter cm = centimeter mm = millimeter

1. Eric can throw a ball about 2,300 cm. How many meters can he throw the ball?

   ____

2. Barbara's book is 30 mm thick. How many centimeters thick is the book?

   ____

3. Delores can reach 2 meters high. How many centimeters can she reach?

   ____

4. Holly can take a giant step of 960 mm. How many centimeters can she step?

   ____

5. We walked 3,000 meters in the shopping mall. How many kilometers did we walk?

   ____

6. Rae Ann is 1,540 mm tall. How many centimeters tall is she?

   ____

Circle the answer that makes the most sense.

1. On our trip downtown and back, we drove the car 40 _______ .

   mm cm m km

2. A city block is 120 _______ long.

   mm cm m km

3. My 8-year-old sister, Diana, is 143 _______ tall.

   mm cm m km

4. Rodney has a handspan of about 14 _______ wide.

   mm cm m km

5. A fly has a wingspan of about 8 _______ wide.

   mm cm m km

6. An acorn is about 1 _______ wide.

   mm cm m km

7. A drinking fountain is about 1 _______ high.

   mm cm m km

Measurement

U.S. Customary Length

Name ______________________

Football Team Workout

As Ms. Parrish's class watched the high school football team, they wrote these math problems about the team and the field. Refer to the chart to answer the questions below.

1 mile = 1760 yards	mi. = mile
1 mile = 5280 feet	yd. = yard
1 yard = 36 inches	ft. = foot
12 inches = 1 foot	in. = inch

1. Jo Anne's brother threw the ball 27 yds. How many ft. did he throw the ball?

____

2. The football field was 100 yds. long. How many ft. long was the field?

____

3. The football field was 162 ft. wide. How many yds. wide was the field?

____

4. The team missed a first down by 1/3 of a yd. How many in. was that?

____

5. The football is 11 in. in length. At least how many footballs would have to be placed end to end to equal more than a yd.?

____

6. The pass receivers practiced 40 yd. sprints. How many feet did they run each time? How many inches?

____

Circle the answer that makes the most sense.

1. A baseball bat is about 3 _______ long.
   inches feet yards miles
2. A ball point pen is about 6 _______ long.
   inches feet yards miles
3. A stepladder is about 6 _______ tall.
   inches feet yards miles
4. The distance around a large pond is about 3 _______ .
   inches feet yards miles
5. A bathtub is about 1 _______ wide.
   inch foot yard mile

Measurement

Name ____________________

Metric Capacity

How Much? How Full?

Jana and her friends wrote some problems about capacity in metric terms. Refer to the chart to answer the questions below.

1 kiloliter	=	1,000 liters
1 liter	=	1,000 milliliters
kl	=	kiloliter
l	=	liter
ml	=	milliliter

1. Jana found that the fish tank held about 20 liters of water. How many milliliters of water did it hold?

   ____

2. Her teacher asked her to give the fish some vitamins each day. If she gave them 35 milliliters each day, how many milliliters would she give them in a week (Monday through Friday)?

   ____

3. Terri waters 6 plants in the classroom. She gives each of the plants 500 milliliters of water. How many milliliters of water does she need to water all of the plants? How many liters does she use?

   ____

4. Susan took 5 milliliters of cough medicine 4 times a day for one week. How many milliliters of medicine did she take in a day? In seven days?

   ____

5. A truck brings fuel oil to school which is stored in a 12-kiloliter tank. How many liters does the tank hold when it is full?

   ____

Circle the answer that makes the most sense.

1. A drop of water is about 1 _______ of water.

   milliliter　　liter　　kiloliter

2. A water cooler holds about 15 _______ of water.

   milliliters　　liters　　kiloliters

3. A milk transport truck tank holds about 12 _______ of milk.

   milliliters　　liters　　kiloliters

4. A single can holds about 340 _______ of soda.

   milliliters　　liters　　kiloliters

5. A bucket of paint holds about 4 _______ of paint.

   milliliters　　liters　　kiloliters

Measurement

Name ____________________

U.S. Customary Capacity

Liquid Refreshment

Kerri is in charge of the fruit punch at the PTO thank-you tea. She has only a one-cup measure. Using the chart, help her change the recipe to cups.

1 gallon = 4 quarts 1 quart = 2 pints 1 pint = 2 cups 1 cup = 8 ounces	gal. = gallon qt. = quart pt. = pint oz. = ounce c. = cup

1. The recipe calls for 2 quarts of water. How many cups of water should she use?

   ____

2. It calls for 16 ounces of frozen lemonade and 8 oz. frozen orange juice. How many total cups of lemonade and orange juice are in the recipe?

   ____

3. The water and frozen juice are mixed with 2 quarts of pineapple juice. How many cups of pineapple juice will she mix in?

   ____

4. Next, she must add 4 quarts of ginger ale. How many cups are in 4 qts.?

   ____

5. How many cups of carbonated water should she add if the recipe calls for 2 quarts?

   ____

6. Finally, 2 cups of sugar are added to the mixture. How many total cups of ingredients have been used in the punch?

   ____

7. Kerri added ice and poured the punch into 4 1/4-quart pitchers. If each person at the tea was served about 1/2 cup of punch, how many people will this recipe serve? (Remember, the sugar dissolves.)

   ____

Circle the answer that makes the most sense.

1. A can of motor oil is about 1 _______ .

   cup   pint   quart   gallon

2. A glass of orange juice is about 1 _______ .

   cup   pint   quart   gallon

3. A large bucket of paint is about 1 _______ .

   cup   pint   quart   gallon

Measurement

Metric Mass

Name ______________________________

How Much Does It Weigh?

The students in Mrs. Penny's fifth grade classroom brought in a collection of things to weigh. Using the chart, answer the questions below.

1 kilogram = 1,000 grams 1 gram = 1,000 milligrams	kilogram = kg gram = g milligram = mg

1. Beverly brought a tennis ball to school. If it weighed 60 grams, how many milligrams would 3 tennis balls weigh?

   ____

2. Aaron brought a can of chicken soup that weighed 360 grams. Would 3 cans of soup weigh over or under 1 kilogram?

   ____

3. Rachel brought a troll doll that weighed 100 grams. About how many from her collection would make a kilogram of troll dolls?

   ____

4. Steven's hair comb weighed 35 grams. How many mg does his comb weigh?

   ____

5. Emily brought a peanut that weighed 8 grams. How many grams would 100 peanuts weigh?

   ____

6. One of Harold's shoes weighed about 500 grams. How many kg would both of his shoes weigh?

   ____

Circle the answer that makes the most sense.

1. A city phone book probably weighs about 2 _______ .

   milligrams grams kilograms

2. A medium-sized apple has the mass of about 175 _______ .

   milligrams grams kilograms

3. A postage stamp probably has a mass of 50 _______ .

   milligrams grams kilograms

4. A chalkboard eraser has a mass of about 50 _______ .

   milligrams grams kilograms

5. A new pencil weighs about 5 _______ .

   milligrams grams kilograms

Measurement

U.S. Customary Weight

Name ______________________

Vegetable Stand

Cary worked at the farmers' market last summer, weighing and selling fruits and vegetables. Using the chart, answer the questions below.

1 ton = 2,000 pounds 1 pound = 16 ounces	ton = t. pound = lb. ounce = oz.

1. Cary's father drove a truck to the farmers' market that could carry 2,000 lbs. of fruits and vegetables. How many tons could his truck carry?

   ____

2. Green beans were $1.19 per pound. If a woman bought 4 pounds, how much change would she get back from a $5 bill?

   ____

3. One man bought 1/2 pound of endive. How many ounces did he buy?

   ____

4. Cary's dad had a special on cantaloupe at $.25 per pound. Cary's friend bought 2 cantaloupes. If his total was $1, how many pounds of cantaloupe did he buy?

   ____

5. On Saturday, Cary gave away a free recycling sticker for every customer who brought their own bag. He gave away 263 stickers. If the average customer who recycles buys 4 pounds of produce, how many pounds of food did they probably sell?

   ____

6. Cary's dad recently put a new top and cover on the stand. The top and cover weighed 1/2 ton. How many pounds did the top and cover weigh?

   ____

Circle the answer that makes the most sense.

1. A rhinoceros may weigh 2 _______ .

   ounces pounds tons

2. A bowling ball weighs about 16 _______ .

   ounces pounds tons

3. A regular sack of flour weighs 5 _______ .

   ounces pounds tons

4. A baseball weighs 5 _______ .

   ounces pounds tons

Measurement

Temperature Celsius

Name ______________________

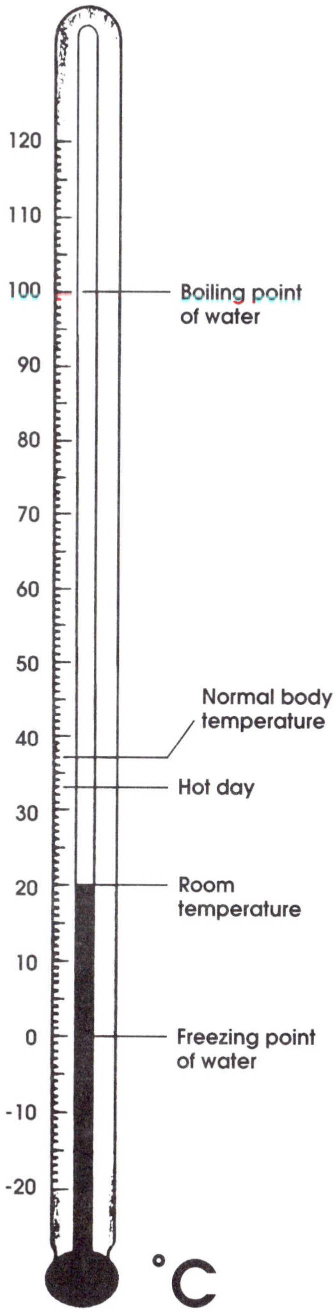

Weather Forecast

Karla did her science fair project on weather forecasting. She recorded the temperature daily in degrees Celsius. Answer her questions in complete sentences.

1. The average temperature in January was 10°C. The average temperature in February was 6°C higher than in January. What was the average temperature in February?

   ____

2. It was cold enough for Karla to go ice skating outside on January 24. Did she record the temperature as -15°C, or 15°C?

   ____

3. Karla filled a hot water bottle with boiling water to take along to warm her hands while she skated. When she started, how many degrees higher was the water in the bottle than the temperature outside?

   ____

4. What clothing should Karla have worn outside when the temperature was -15°C?

   ____

5. One day, Karla had a body temperature of 40°C. Was she well or sick?

   ____

6. The average temperature in March, according to Karla's weather station, was 22°C. Using the temperatures from problem one, what was the average temperature between January, February, and March?

   ____

7. Karla read in the newspaper that the average temperature in her city for August was 32°C. How much higher was the average temperature in August than in January?

   ____

8. Karla's mother thought the refrigerator was breaking down. Karla used her thermometer to check the temperature inside the refrigerator. Should it have read -5°C or 5°C?

   ____

Picture Graph

Name ____________________

After-School Activities

The school newspaper editors at Bluebird Lane School encouraged students to take part in after-school activities. They published this picture graph. Refer to the graph to answer each question.

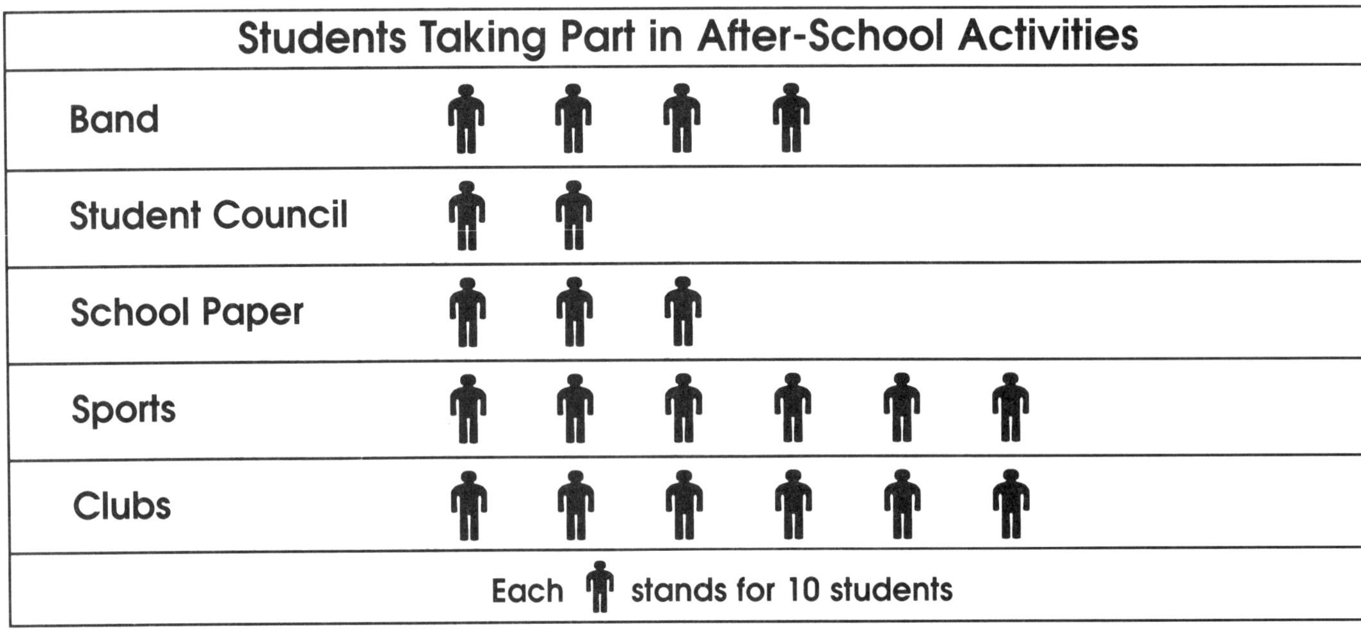

____

1. How many total students take part in after-school activities?

2. In which two activities do the greatest number of students take part?

3. How many more students take part in sports than in the band?

4. Which activity represented has the least participation?

5. How many fewer students take part in the student council than the school paper?

6. What is the title of the picture graph?

7. The picture graph should show when the graph was made and who made it. Please add "Bluebird School paper" and the current year to the bottom of the graph.

Bar Graph

Name ______________________

Vowel Search

Janet was helping out in the first grade. The children were learning to recognize the vowels. The children counted each vowel in a newspaper clipping. Janet made this bar graph to show the results. Refer to the graph to answer the following questions.

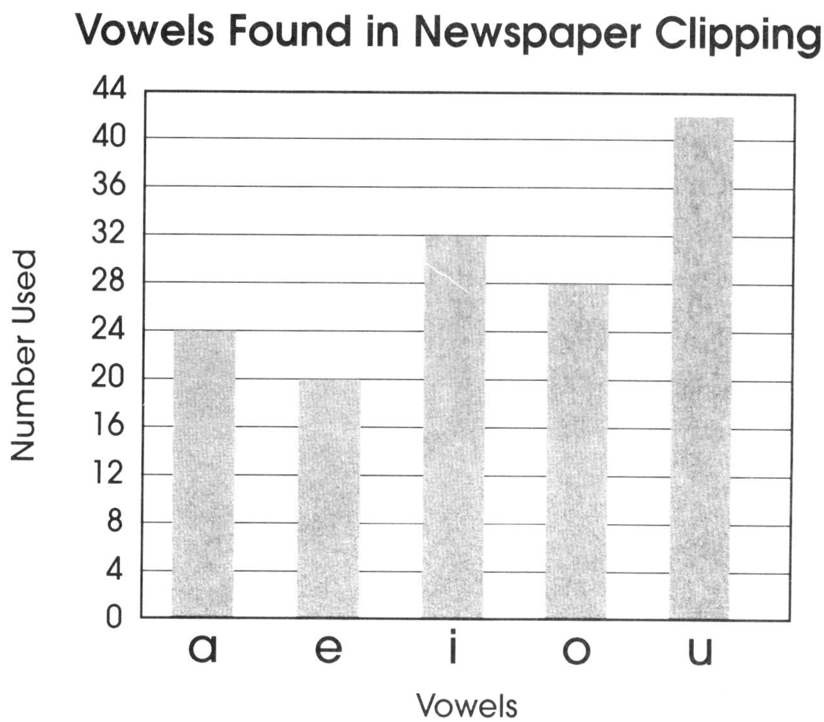

1. How many vowels did the children find all together?
____
2. How many more times was "i" found than "e"?
____
3. How many fewer times was "a" found than "o"?
____
4. What does it mean when the bar for the "u" stops between lines?
____
5. On another paper, make a bar graph to show the number of times different vowels are used in your first, middle, and last name. Write two sentences that explain your graph.
____
____
____
____

Circle Graph

Name ____________________

Ned's Allowance

Ned earned an allowance of $10.00 each week. He created this circle graph on his computer to show his parents how he spent it. Refer to the circle graph to answer each question below.

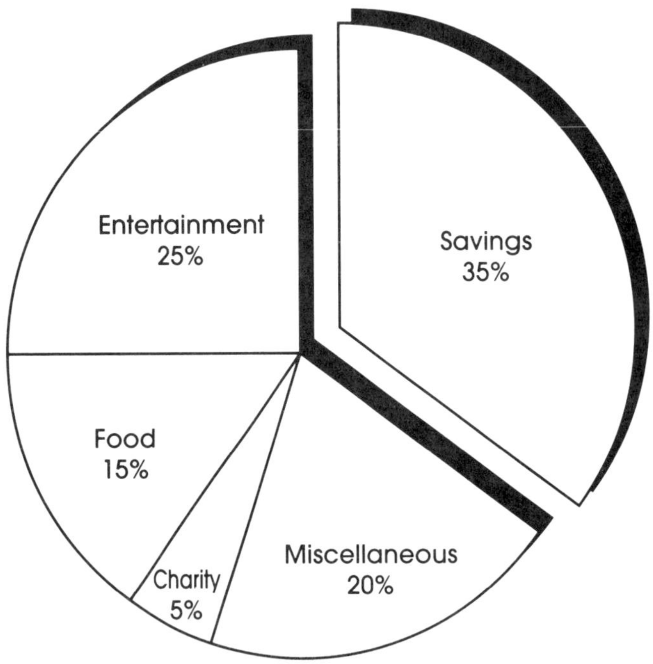

1. Ned highlighted the savings segment of the circle graph because his family believed that having a savings account was very important. If Ned saved $3.50 each week, how much would be left of his allowance for other things?

   ____

2. Ned spends all of his entertainment allowance on movies. How much does he spend each week on movies?

   ____

3. How much does Ned spend each week on miscellaneous expenses? Name some things he might buy which would fall into this category.

   ____

4. If you have an allowance, create your own circle graph detailing your spending habits. If you don't have an allowance, write two sentences describing how you would spend $10.00 differently than Ned.

   ____

   ____

Line Graph

Name ______________________

Library Lending Curve

While the local library was being remodeled last year from January to June, it was open only from 9 A.M. until 10 A.M. each day. The librarian prepared this line graph to show how many books were checked out during this period and after the remodeling was complete. Refer to the line graph to answer the questions below.

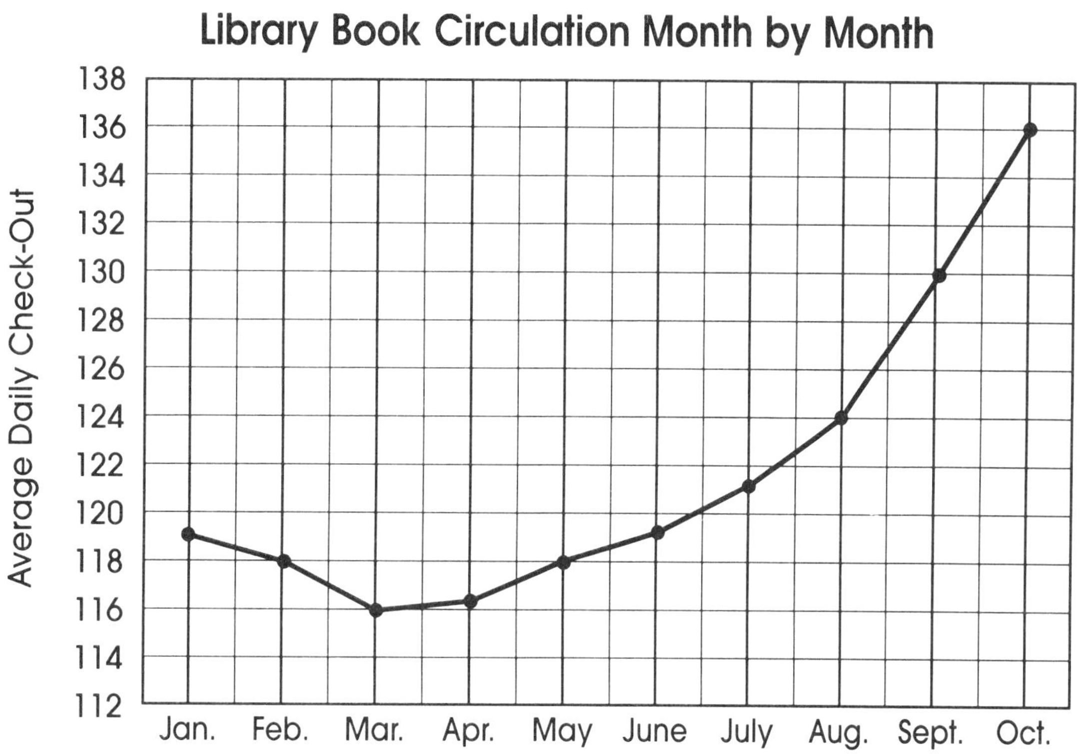

1. How many books, on average, were checked out daily in January? List the months that had a lower daily check-out rate than January.

   ____

2. Were more books checked out in August and September or in July and August?

   ____

3. Which two months had the greatest number of books checked out daily?

   ____

4. What does it mean when a month shows a dot between the grid lines?

   ____

5. What is the average number of books checked out daily from January to October?

   ____

Answer Key

Math Word Problems

Grade 5

Place Value Name ____________

Dizzy Digits

Read the clues and write each number described.

1. It has 9 digits. All the digits are 0 except one 6. What is the number?
   600,000,000
2. If you reverse the digits on this three-digit number, it will have 4 hundreds, 9 tens and 7 ones. What is the original number?
   794
3. The digits of this number are in sequential order. If you add the four digits together, they add up to 10. None of the digits are zero. What is the number?
   1,234
4. List all the different four-digit numbers that use the digits 4, 4, 5, and 5.
   4,455; 5,544; 4,545; 5,454; 5,445; 4,554
5. All the digits are the same in this five-digit number. The sum of the digits is 30. What is the number?
   66,666
6. Use each of the digits 1 through 8 to make two four-digit numbers. Arrange to give the greatest possible sum when the two numbers are added together.
   8642 + 7531 = 16,173 Answers may vary slightly
7. If you reverse the digits on this five-digit number, it will have 9 ten-thousands, 4 thousands, 8 hundreds, and 1 one. What is the number?
   10,849
8. List the different numbers that follow, using these clues. The number of hundreds plus the number of thousands is 2. The number of tens is 3 times the number of thousands. The number of ones is 2 times the number of hundreds.
   1,132 ; 0,204 ; 2,060
9. Write the largest five-digit number possible using any digits 1 through 9. No digit may be used more than once.
   98,765

Page 1

Addition Name ____________
With Renaming

The Great Calorie Count

Everyone in Marjorie's family counted calories to maintain a healthy weight. Read about their meals and write the number of calories calculated.

1. Marjorie made a sandwich for her school lunch. She used 2 slices of bread at 58 calories each. She spread 1 tablespoon of margarine on the bread at 101 calories. She added 1 slice of cheese at 101 calories, and a slice of lunch meat at 161 calories. How many calories were in her sandwich?
   479 calories
2. Along with her sandwich, Marjorie ate a pear with 101 calories. She also bought a half-pint of milk with 152 calories. How many calories were in her whole lunch?
   732 calories
3. Her brother George packed his lunch with two chicken legs with 209 calories each, a container of applesauce at 116 calories, a celery stick at 7 calories and a cookie at 96 calories. How many calories were in George's lunch?
   637 calories
4. For breakfast, Marjorie, her brother, and her parents each had a dish of oatmeal at 130 calories, a glass of milk at 150 calories, and a half-cup of raisins at 210 calories. How many breakfast calories did they all have together?
   1,960 calories for 4 people
5. For dinner, each family member ate a serving of roast beef at 393 calories, corn on the cob at 242 calories, with margarine at 101 calories. They had green beans at 17 calories, a salad at 52 calories, with dressing at 41 calories. They each had a glass of milk at 150 calories. Their mother said they could have dessert if they each stayed under 1,000 calories for the whole meal. Will they get dessert? Explain.
   yes, each meal totaled 996 calories, less than 1,000.
6. For dessert they each had chocolate ice cream at 220 calories and a slice of cake with 320 calories. How many calories were in each dessert?
   540 calories
7. How many calories did Marjorie eat today for breakfast, lunch, and dinner combined?
   b 490 cal. l 732 cal. d 996. total: 2,218 cal.
   with dessert, 2,758 cal

USE YOUR CALCULATOR
How many total calories did the four people in Marjorie's family eat for dinner and dessert?
996 + 540 × 4 total = 6144 calories

Page 2

Addition Name ____________
With Regrouping

When I Grow Up

The upper grades at Glenridge School were studying different jobs. Speakers at a job fair taught them about the costs involved in various jobs. Calculate the costs described.

1. Louis's father came to talk about his music store. He showed the students a saxophone for \$719.95, a clarinet for \$859.95, and a flute for \$825.95. If the school band bought all three instruments, how much would they spend?
   \$ 2405.85
2. Bob's mother is a photographer. She brought in her equipment and talked about events she had photographed. She described one job for which she spent \$60 for film, \$75 for developing the film, and \$85 in other expenses. How much did it cost her to photograph that event?
   \$220.00
3. David's father, a traveling salesman, flies to different cities to sell his products. In one month he flew to Atlanta for \$239, to New Orleans for \$349, and to Dallas for \$431. How much did he have to spend on airfare that month?
   \$ 1,019.00
4. Tim's mother is a landscaper. On a new home in the neighborhood, she spent \$829 for trees, \$358 for flowers, and \$352 for a fish pond. How much did she spend on items for the new yard?
   \$ 1,539.00
5. The children asked their teacher, Mr. Thompson, if he had any expenses. He explained that, among other things, he took a class last summer. It cost him \$515 for tuition, \$49 for a book, and \$29 for other expenses (pens, paper, etc.). How much did Mr. Thompson spend for summer school?
   \$ 593.00
6. Tori's father, a policeman, came to school to talk about his job. The students asked him to list some of his expenses. He spent \$239 for a uniform, \$219 for his gun, \$198 for his jacket, and \$49 for his handcuffs. How much did it cost to outfit himself?
   \$ 705.00
7. Beverly's father is an auto repairman. When he visited, he said that his expenses included tools, which cost \$2,500, a cart to slide under the cars for \$149, and \$59 for his uniform. What was the total of these expenses?
   \$ 2,708.00

USE YOUR CALCULATOR
The students made a book detailing the expenses of various jobs. The students spent \$17 on paper for the book, \$25 on magic markers, and \$3 for pencils. What was the total of their expenses?
\$ 45.00

They produced 25 copies of the book with those supplies. What was the average cost of each book?
\$1.80 per book

Page 3

Subtraction Name ____________
With Renaming

Meet Me at the Fair

In 1904, the world's fair in St. Louis caused much wonder among people. New inventions, foods, and art sparked interest throughout the world. Read about the fair and calculate the problems.

1. Peanut butter was introduced at the world's fair in 1904. The first commercial peanut butter was produced by a St. Louis doctor in 1890. How long after its production was it introduced at the fair?
   14 years
2. The largest Ferris wheel was built for the Chicago Fair in 1893. The same Ferris wheel was used at the St. Louis world's fair in 1904, then torn down and sold for scrap in 1904. How many years did the Ferris wheel run?
   11 years
3. No one is sure where ice cream was first made, but the ice cream cone was first used at the world's fair in 1904. How many years has it been since we first used the cone to hold ice cream?
   Answers will vary. Present year − 1904 =
4. What year will be the 100th anniversary of the 1904 world's fair?
   2004
5. The hot dog was also introduced at the world's fair in 1904. Carla ate her first hot dog in 1987. How many years after the hot dog was introduced did Carla eat her first one?
   83 years
6. Approximately 10,984,000 men and approximately 8,927,000 women came to the St. Louis world's fair. How many more men than women visited the fair?
   2,057,000 more men
7. Special buildings were constructed in 1903 to hold displays at the world's fair. How many years old are these buildings now?
   Answers will vary. Present year − 1903 =
8. The U.S. flag had fewer stars in 1904, but had 13 stripes just as it does today. If 7 of these stripes are red, how many are white?
   6 white stripes

USE YOUR CALCULATOR
It is estimated that 450,000 incandescent lights were used at the 1904 world's fair. Thomas Edison perfected the incandescent lamp in 1879. How many years later were so many of them used at the fair?
25 years later

Page 4

Subtraction Name ____________
With Renaming

The Rock Concert

Cindy's older sister took her to see her favorite rock band at the Fox Theater. Read about their evening and answer the questions in complete sentences.

1. How old was Cindy? The concert was in July of 1995. She was born in June of 1984.
   Cindy was 11 years old.
2. They left for the concert at 5:30 P.M. They arrived at 7:30 P.M. How long did it take them to drive?
   It took them 2 hours to get to the concert
3. There were 3,030 seats in the two-level Fox Theater. If 1,275 of the seats were on the ground level, how many were in the balcony?
   There were 1755 seats in the balcony.
4. Earlier that week, her mother had bought Cindy a special outfit to wear to the concert. It cost \$43.89. If Mother handed the clerk a \$50.00 bill, how much change did she get?
   Mother received \$6.11 in change.
5. They had a wonderful time. The concert lasted from 8:00 P.M. until 11:30 P.M. How long was the concert?
   The concert lasted 3½ hours.
6. The feature band played on the stage for 2 hours and 15 minutes. How much of the total concert time did that band not play?
   The feature band did not play for 1hr. 15min.
7. Before the feature band, a "warm-up" band played. How long did the warm-up band play?
   They must have played for 1hr. 15min.
8. Cindy bought a souvenir T-shirt after the concert. Of the 3,020 people who attended the concert, 243 bought T-shirts. How many did not buy a T-shirt?
   2,777 people did not buy a T-shirt.
9. Cindy also bought a CD for \$16.95. If she gave the clerk a \$20.00 bill, what was her change?
   She received \$3.05 in change.

USE YOUR CALCULATOR
The odometer on the family car read 39,871 when the two sisters left their driveway at 5:30 that night. It read 40,082 when they got home after the concert. How many total miles did they drive that evening?
They drove 211 miles that evening.

Page 5

Addition and Subtraction Name ____________
With Renaming

Halloween Party

When Miguel and Anita planned a Halloween party, they encountered many numbers. Help them solve the equations.

1. The room which they planned to use was 20 feet by 30 feet. What was the perimeter of the room?
   100 feet
2. If they needed enough crepe paper to go around the perimeter of the room twice, how many feet of crepe paper should they buy?
   200 feet
3. Miguel bought a box of 50 invitations. They sent an invitation to 25 girls and 23 boys. How many invitations were left over?
   2 invitations left
4. They bought a Halloween party kit for \$13.50, 5 pumpkins for \$2.00 each, and 10 candles for \$1.00 each. How much money did they spend on these party supplies?
   \$33.50
5. It took Anita 1 hour and 15 minutes to carve each jack-o'-lantern. How long did she spend carving the five jack-o'-lanterns?
   6 hrs. 15min.
6. Their friend Carlos bought a ghost costume for \$4.50 and a jack-o'-lantern flashlight for \$3.25. How much did Carlos spend all together?
   \$ 7.75
7. Another friend, Lupita, bought 2 yards of orange cloth at \$1.59 per yard and a package of elastic for \$.98. Using those materials, her mother made a jack-o'-lantern costume for Lupita and stuffed it with newspaper. How much did her costume cost?
   \$ 4.16
8. The children bought 108 apples. They made 50 candied apples and used the rest for the game, *Bobbing for Apples*. How many apples did they use for the game?
   58 apples
9. After the party, Juan won the prize for the best costume. He came as a broom. He wrapped his upper body in black crepe paper and wore a straw skirt around his hips. The crepe paper was \$.49 and the straw skirt was \$.69. How much did the walking broom spend on his costume?
   \$ 1.18

USE YOUR CALCULATOR
After the party, everyone helped Anita and Miguel clean up. There were 48 guests at the party, and each person spent 30 minutes cleaning up. How many combined hours did it take to help clean up?
24 combined hours

Page 6

Multiplication and Division Name ____________

Flight

The Young Eagle's club made an informational book about airplanes to show their classmates what they were learning. Complete each problem they proposed.

1. Roy read about the first airplane made by the Wright brothers. It reached 30 miles per hour on its first flight. If a small, propeller-driven, single-engine plane flies about 5 times this fast, at what speed can it fly?
   150 mph
2. Amy's father is a pilot on a jet airliner. He flies from Chicago to Los Angeles, a distance of 2,000 miles. If the jet flew at 500 miles per hour, how long would it take him to fly from Chicago to Los Angeles?
   4 hours
3. Last summer, Barbara's family flew in a four-engine propeller plane from Chicago to Glacier National Park. It took them 3 hours. If the plane flew 400 miles per hour, how many miles was it from Chicago to Glacier National Park?
   1,200 miles
4. The supersonic transport travels 1,500 miles per hour. If it takes 2 hours to fly from New York to London, how many miles is the flight between these cities?
   3,000 miles
5. If a twin engine jet flies about 500 miles an hour, which plane described above travels about 3 times as fast?
   the supersonic transport
6. Most people choose to fly on the jumbo jet. If it travels at 600 miles per hour, how long would it take to travel the 3,000 miles from New York to London?
   5 hours
7. How long would it take to fly the 3,000 miles from New York to London in a twin-engine jet if it flies 500 miles per hour?
   6 hours
8. The Wright brothers' plane could never have flown the 3,000 miles from New York to London, but if it had been possible to fly that far at 30 miles per hour, how long would it have taken?
   100 hours

USE YOUR CALCULATOR
Lee took a trip with his uncle, who flies a small, single-engine, propeller plane. They flew 4 hours from Chicago to Atlanta, then 4 more hours to Miami. If the plane flies 150 miles per hour, how many miles did they fly from Chicago to Miami?
1,200 miles

Page 7

Multiplication

Name ____________

Zoo Information

Mrs. Carson's class gathered information about African animals from the zoo. They came back to school with the following problems. Answer in complete sentences.

1. Each tiger at the zoo eats about 85 pounds of meat in a week. How many pounds of meat must the zoo provide each week for the 14 tigers it owns?
   They must provide about 1,190 pounds of meat.
2. The baby gorilla at the zoo weighed only 5 pounds at birth. Its father weighed 90 times as much. How much did the father gorilla weigh?
   Its father weighs about 450 lbs.
3. If an elephant eats about 95 pounds of food a day, how much food will the elephant eat in a year?
   It eats about 34,675 lbs a year. (except leap year)
4. Each hyena eats about 3 pounds of food a day. How many pounds of food will a pack of 15 hyenas need for 31 days?
   The pack of hyenas will need about 1,395 lbs.
5. A hippopotamus requires about 50 pounds of food per day to maintain its weight. How much does it weigh if its weight is about 110 times its daily food intake?
   The hippo weighs about 5,500 lbs.
6. An average lion eats about 75 pounds of meat at a time. It eats about 3 times a week. About how many pounds of meat will it eat in one year?
   Each year, the lion eats about 11,700 lbs.
7. A large antelope called the eland stands about 6 feet tall. It can stretch its neck and eat from the tops of trees which are 1.5 times taller. How tall are these trees?
   The trees are around 9 ft. tall.
8. A baby elephant may weigh about 250 pounds at birth. By the time it is an adult, it weighs 50 times as much. How much does the adult elephant weigh?
   The adult elephant weighs about 12,500 lbs.

USE YOUR CALCULATOR

Each ostrich needs a pen about 20 feet by 10 feet. How many square feet of space will be needed by 11 ostriches?

Eleven ostriches need about 2,200 square feet.

Page 8

Multiplication

Name ____________

Running a Truck Farm

Mark lives on a farm where he and his family raise fruits and vegetables and ship them to market by truck. Read about the farm and answer the questions in complete sentences.

1. They planted 98 rows of corn with 125 plants in each row. How many corn plants did they plant?
   They planted 12,250 corn plants.
2. While picking peaches, they filled 742 bushel baskets. Each basket held 45 peaches. How many peaches did they pick?
   They picked 33,390 peaches.
3. 41 plums were packed in 1-peck cartons. If there were 237 cartons, how many plums were packed?
   9,717 plums were packed into 1-peck cartons.
4. The truck made deliveries in a 191-kilometer route each day for 23 days of the busiest month. How many total kilometers did the truck travel in that one month?
   The truck traveled 4,393 kilometers that month.
5. The family picked 15 cartons of green beans daily. If each case held about 300 green beans, about how many green beans did they pick?
   The family picked 4,500 beans daily.
6. When the cantaloupes were ripe, they shipped 430 cases each day. If a case held 12 cantaloupes, how many cantaloupes were shipped each day?
   5,160 cantaloupes were shipped each day.
7. Mark's father works an average of 48 hours a week. If he works 45 weeks of the year, about how many hours does he work in a year?
   Mark's father works about 2,160 hours/year.
8. Mark gets paid $3.00 for each case of corn he picks. If he picked 27 cases of corn last week, how much money did he earn?
   Mark earned $81 last week.
9. Mark's brother John drives the tractor which plants the crops. He gets paid $9.50 per hour. If he worked 48 hours this week, how much would he be paid?
   Mark's brother would be paid $456 this week.

USE YOUR CALCULATOR

One grocery store that sells this produce serves an average of 349 customers each day. The store is open 364 days a year. About how many people come to the store in a year?

127,036 people come to the store each year.

Page 9

Mixed Operations

Add, Subtract, Multiply

Name ____________

The Fishing Trip

Emily and her family take a fishing trip in the mountains each year. Read about their preparations and circle whether to **add**, to **subtract**, or to **multiply**. Write the numerical answer on the correct line.

1. The family bought a large tent for $79.95. They also purchased an ice chest for $11.89. They bought two fuel tanks for the cook stove at $5.00 each. What did they spend altogether for these camping supplies?
   Add $101.84 Subtract ______ Multiply ______
2. The three children had outgrown their hiking boots. Boots were on sale for $24.50 each. How much did the three pairs of hiking boots cost?
   Add ______ Subtract ______ Multiply $73.50
3. Last year, the food for the 10-day trip cost $259.82. This year, they spent only $186.89 on food. How much less did they spend this year?
   Add ______ Subtract $72.93 Multiply ______
4. Each of their six water bottles holds 8 gallons. How many gallons of water did they take?
   Add ______ Subtract ______ Multiply 48 gal.
5. Emily bought 6 new fishing lures. They were $.59, $.89, $.79, $.39, $.69, and $.65. How much did she pay in total for the lures?
   Add $4 Subtract ______ Multiply ______
6. Emily's mother bought two bottles of sunscreen for $2.39 each, and two bottles of insect spray for $1.29. How much did she spend on protection from sun and insects?
   Add $7.36 Subtract ______ Multiply 4.78 2.58
7. The fee for camping at the campsite was $6.50 per day. If the family camped there for 10 days, how much did they pay to camp?
   Add ______ Subtract ______ Multiply $65

USE YOUR CALCULATOR

The altitude at their home was 3,850 feet. The altitude at their campsite was 9,875 feet. How much higher was the altitude at the campsite than at their home?

Add ______ Subtract 6025 ft. Multiply ______

Page 10

Division

Name ____________

Service Station Employee

Samantha's big brother, Bert, works at a service station. Read about his job and write each answer in a complete sentence.

1. The service station has a supply of 95 tires. How many sets of 4 tires can be sold from this supply?
   They can sell 23 sets of tires.
2. If 4 tires cost $259, how much does one tire cost?
   One tire costs $64.75
3. The service station made $207.00 changing oil in one day. If they changed the oil for 9 cars, how much did each oil change cost?
   Each oil change costs $23.
4. Samantha's father filled up his car with $9.81 of gasoline. If he got 9 gallons of gasoline, how much did gas cost per gallon?
   Gas costs $1.09 per gallon.
5. Bert counted the service station's supply of spark plugs. Each car takes 4 spark plugs, and he counted 84 spark plugs. How many cars can they service with spark plugs before they need to reorder?
   They have enough for 21 cars.
6. The service station made $315 one week on car washes. If each car wash cost $7, how many cars were washed that week?
   They washed 45 cars that week.
7. Bert makes $35 per day for working at the service station. If he gets paid $5 per hour, how many hours does he work in a day?
   Bert works 7 hours a day.
8. During the summer, when Bert isn't in school, he makes $700 a month. If he is paid $35 per day, how many days per month does he work in the summer?
   He works 20 days per month.
9. Bert wants to buy a car that costs $2,000. How many days will he have to work to buy the car he wants?
   He will have to work at least 58 days.

USE YOUR CALCULATOR

During the school year, Bert makes $35 on Saturdays. He estimated the expenses for his new car will be about $1,400 for a year. How many Saturdays will he have to work to cover the expenses for his car?

He will have to work at least 40 Saturdays.

Page 11

Division

Name ____________

Preparing for the Prom

Wayne helped his sister who was on the prom preparation committee. She had these problems to solve. Write the answers in complete sentences.

1. The committee hired a band for the dance for $500. If the dance lasts from 8 P.M. until 12 P.M., how much will the band be paid per hour?
   The band will be paid $125 per hour.
2. The dance band has 5 members. How much does each band member get paid per hour?
   Each band member makes $25 per hour.
3. The committee rented 4 special-effects lights for $100. How much would it cost to rent one light?
   One light would cost $25.
4. The committee will rent 256 chairs for the dance. If 4 chairs fit around one table, how many tables will they need to rent?
   They will rent 64 tables.
5. There is a fountain in the middle of the dance floor that holds 150 gallons of water. The committee has a 5-gallon bucket. How many buckets of water will it take to fill the fountain?
   The bucket will need to be filled 30 times.
6. The committee has ordered 192 flowers to be put in vases on the tables. If 3 flowers go in each vase, how many vases will they need?
   They will need 64 vases.
7. Wayne helped his sister put crepe paper around the walls of the room. Each wall was 20 yards long. They used 40 yards of crepe paper per wall. Will 160 yards of crepe paper be enough to decorate the square room?
   Yes, 40 yds per wall times 4 walls equals 160 yds.
8. After the prom was over, a clean up crew of 7 people worked a total of 21 hours to get the room back to order. How many hours did they each work?
   Each person worked 3 hours.

USE YOUR CALCULATOR

The expenses for the prom were $500 for the band, $100 for the lights, $100 for the fountain, $300 for the flowers and vases, and $125 for the crepe paper. If 250 people bought tickets for $5 each, will the prom committee have enough money to cover their expenses?

Costs = 1125 ticket sales = 1250 Yes, they have enough to cover their expenses.

Page 12

Division

Name ____________

Miles per Hour

Mrs. Craig brought some posters to her class from a travel agency. She asked her class to make division problems about travel. Read the problems they wrote and write the answers in complete sentences.

1. If a car traveled at an average speed of 55 miles per hour, how long would it take to go 467.5 miles?
   The car would take 8 1/2 hours to go 467.5 miles.
2. A cruise liner traveled 2,520 miles to reach port in 72 hours. How many miles per hour did the cruise ship travel?
   The ship traveled at 35 mph.
3. A jumbo jet traveled 2,400 miles from Chicago to Mexico in 4 hours. How many miles per hour was it flying?
   The jet was flying at 600 mph.
4. An express train averaged 70 miles per hour. About how long did it take this train to travel from Chicago to Kansas City, a distance of 665 miles?
   The train took 9 1/2 hours from Chicago to K.C.
5. If the express train traveled 777 miles from Kansas City to Albuquerque at 70 miles per hour, how many hours would it take to get to Albuquerque?
   It would take 11.1 hours.
6. The distance from Chicago to San Diego is about 2,500 miles. If you wanted to plan an 8-day trip one way, how many miles would you have to drive each day?
   You would drive 312.5 miles each day.
7. If the moon were about 236,952 miles from Earth, and a rocket ship could take you there in 72 hours, how many miles per hour would you be averaging?
   The ship would have to travel at 3,291 mph.

USE YOUR CALCULATOR

The Pony Express ran from St. Joseph, MO, to Sacramento, CA. The riders took 10 days to cover 1,966 miles. If they rode 196.6 miles per day (riding 24 hours a day), how many miles per hour did the Pony Express riders average?

They averaged 8.2 mph.

Page 13

Finding Averages

Name ____________

Class Averages

Mrs. Corrigan helped her students figure their average score on the tests they took. Read about the various scores and write a complete answer.

1. Out of 100 points possible on the first math test, the total for 24 students was 2,064 points. What was the class average? Emily made 94 points on the test. Was Emily above or below average?
   The class average was 86 points. Emily was above average.
2. If Bob made 58 points on the same test, was he above or below average?
   Bob was below the class average.
3. On the second math test, the total for 23 students was 2,047 points. Ken was not present for the test. When he made it up, above what number did he have to score to be above average?
   Ken would have to score above 89 points.
4. On the third test, the total for 24 students was 1,824 points. If Darnell's score was 82, did he make a score above or below average?
   Darnell's score was above the class average of 76 pts.
5. Mrs. Corrigan provided her class with some more practice on division with 2-digit divisors, and she gave them the third test again. This time their total points equaled 2,040 for 24 students. What was their average this time? By how much did their average improve?
   This time the average was 85 pts. They improved by 9 pts.
6. She threw out the lowest score for each student, and averaged the three remaining scores. The test averages were 86, 89, and 85. What is the overall average for the first quarter grade?
   The overall average was 86.67 points.
7. The science tests were averaged the same way. Ms. Molecule totaled 2,184 points for her 24 students on the first test. If Bill had a score of 87, was he above or below average?
   Bill's score fell below the class average of 91 pts.
8. On the second science test, the 24 students earned a total of 2,232 points. What was the class average for test two?
   The class average was 93 pts.
9. On the third science test, 24 students earned a total of 2,040 points. What was the average score? Do you think the students were more prepared for this science test than for the third math test?
   Average = 89.2 pts. Since the average was better than the 3rd math test they were probably better prepared.

USE YOUR CALCULATOR

Anyone in the class with a 92 average or better got an A. Yakira had scores in Math of 91, 93 and 97. Did Yakira get an A?

Yakira got an A because her average was 93.67.

Page 14

Mixed Operations

Add, Subtract, Multiply, and Divide

Name ____________

Skate-A-Thon

The fifth grade of Honeywell School sponsored a Skate-A-Thon to help raise money for a local children's hospital. Read each problem. Circle whether to **add**, **subtract**, **multiply**, or **divide**. Write the answer to the question on the correct line.

1. Gregory's father was the director for the Skate-A-Thon. He required that each child bring their own skates and safety helmets. 37 of 42 students who entered the event already had skates, and 20 had a helmet. How many students needed to buy or rent skates and helmets?
   Add ______ (Subtract) 5 skates 22 helmets Multiply ______ Divide ______
2. Marianne saved $10 a week from babysitting to pay for new skates and a helmet. She paid $45 for skates and $25 for a helmet. How many weeks did she have to save $10?
   (Add) $70 Subtract ______ Multiply ______ (Divide) 7 weeks
3. Elizabeth decided her skate wheels were worn out. She paid $19.90 for a new set. How much change did she get back from a $20.00 bill?
   Add ______ (Subtract) $.10 Multiply ______ Divide ______
4. For five days, the students practiced in a local roller rink to get in shape for the Skate-A-Thon. It cost each child $1.75 per day to get into the rink. How much did 42 students pay in all?
   Add ______ Subtract ______ (Multiply) $367.50 Divide ______
5. The students asked people to pledge $.50 for every mile they skated. If Orlando skated 16 miles, how much money would he collect?
   Add ______ Subtract ______ (Multiply) $8 Divide ______
6. The park in which they held the Skate-A-Thon had one 4-mile paved trail and one 8-mile paved trail. What route might a student take who wanted to skate 12 miles? List different possibilities.
   Four mile route 3 times, 8 mile + 4 mile route

USE YOUR CALCULATOR

If each student skated an average of 14 miles, how many miles did 42 students skate?

Forty-two students skated 588 miles.

How much money did they raise for the hospital at $.50 per mile?

They raised $294 for the hospital.

Page 15

Decimals

Addition and Subtraction

Name ____________

Vitamin C

For her science fair project, Maggie wanted to see if taking vitamin C helped ward off colds. She asked her friends to help her by keeping track of the amount of vitamin C they took each day. Each friend was supposed to take in at least 60 percent of the recommended daily allowance (RDA) of vitamin C for breakfast. Write each answer in a complete sentence.

1. Lynn drank 1 glass of orange juice, containing 100% RDA vitamin C, 1 cup of milk, containing 1.84% of vitamin C, and ate 1 cup of corn flakes, containing 25.8% RDA of vitamin C. Did she take 60% of the RDA of vitamin C? How much was she over or under her goal? Yes!
   She took 127.64% which was 67.64% over.
2. Wesley ate a 1/2 cup of strawberries, containing 74.46% of vitamin C, 1 egg, containing 0 vitamin C and 1 piece of toast containing 0 vitamin C. Did he reach his goal of 60% RDA of vitamin C? How much was he under or over his goal?
   Yes, he was 14.46% over his goal.
3. Emily ate 1 cup of raisin flake cereal, with 0% RDA of vitamin C, and 1 cup of milk, with 1.84% RDA of vitamin C. Did she reach her goal? If she had added 1 glass of orange juice at 100% RDA, how much vitamin C would she have had that day?
   No, she didn't reach her goal. With oj, 101.84%
4. Sarah ate 1/2 grapefruit at 62.50% RDA, a piece of toast at 0 mg and hot chocolate at 2.52% RDA of vitamin C. How much was she under or over her goal?
   Sarah was over 5.02%.
5. Brian ate 1/2 cup of strawberries with 74.46% RDA of vitamin C, 1 cup of milk with 1.84% RDA of vitamin C, and 1 cup of raisin flakes cereal with 0 vitamin C. Did he reach his goal? How much was he under or over the goal?
   Yes, Brian was over 16.30%.
6. Which student had the most vitamin C for breakfast?
   Lynn had the most vitamin C for breakfast.
7. Which kind of foods seemed to have the most vitamin C?
   Fruits and juice have the most.

EXTENSION

Did you have 60% or more of the RDA of vitamin C for breakfast today? Use nutritional information on packages or from a cookbook to calculate.

Answers will vary.

Page 16

Decimals
Money

Name ______________

Shopping for Gifts

A group of friends went to the mall to look for gifts for their family and friends at the holiday season. Read about their choices and write complete answers.

1. Heather looked for a pair of silver earrings for her sister. One pair was $19.95, and the other pair was $12.49. How much less did the second pair cost?
   The second pair was $7.46 less.
2. Fred chose a mug for his teacher which cost $4.79. How much change did he get from a $10 bill?
   He received $5.21 in change.
3. Since Lani loved music boxes, she bought one for each of her two sisters. One music box cost $18.59, and the other was $16.99. How much did she spend on music boxes?
   She spent $35.58 on music boxes.
4. Peggy bought some piano sheet music for the holidays. The first piece was $3.39, the second was $2.95, and the third was $4.49. How much did she pay for the three pieces of sheet music?
   She spent $10.83 on sheet music.
5. Bill only brought $20.00 with him. He bought a shirt for his dad for $14.79. Then, he found a sweater for his mother which was on sale for only $9.88. How much would he have to borrow from John to buy the sweater?
   He would have to borrow $4.67 from John.
6. Barry had 3 ten-dollar bills. He wanted to buy his brother a football for $9.95 and a soccer ball for his sister which cost $14.49. Does he have enough money? How much more does he need, or how much change will he get?
   He has enough. His change will be $5.56.
7. While they were shopping, Peggy and Lani stopped for lunch. They each bought a soda at $1.19 each, and they split a hamburger which was $1.49. How much was their lunch bill?
   The total bill was $3.87.
8. Rachel bought a charm for her mother's bracelet. It cost $8.99. Last year she spent only $5.59 on a charm. How much more did the charm cost her this year?
   She spent $3.40 more this year.

USE YOUR CALCULATOR
Rachel's mother gave the children a ride to the mall. When they left home to pick up the children, the car's odometer read 85,661.5. After she took each one back home, the odometer read 85,693.9. How many miles had she driven?
She drove 32.4 miles.

Page 17

Decimals
Thousandths Place

Name ______________

Batting Averages

In baseball, the batting averages are expressed in decimals to the thousandths place. A batting average is the number of hits divided by the number of times a player has been at bat. List these great hitters in order of their batting averages, from most to least. Then answer the questions below.

Ty Cobb	0.367	Rogers Hornsby	0.358
Babe Ruth	0.342	Lou Gehrig	0.340
Joe DiMaggio	0.325	Ted Williams	0.406

Ted Williams	.406
Ty Cobb	.367
Rogers Hornsby	.358
Babe Ruth	.342
Lou Gehrig	.340
Joe DiMaggio	.325

1. How much higher was the average of the man in first place than the man in second place?
   His average was .039 higher.
2. How much lower was the batting average of the man in last place than the man in second place?
   His average was .042 lower
3. Jackie Robinson had a batting average of 0.342. How much lower was his batting average than Ted Williams'?
   Robinson's was .064 lower than T.W.'s.
4. Willie Mays had a batting average of 0.302. How much lower was his than Babe Ruth's average?
   Mays' average was .04 lower than Ruth's.
5. The pitcher for the Eagles had an earned run average of 3.56 last year. The pitcher of the Blue Jays had an average of 4.37. Which pitcher had the greater earned run average? How much greater was it?
   The pitcher for the Blue Jays had a higher average. .81 greater

USE YOUR CALCULATOR
If a team had a winning record of 0.647 one year, 0.740 the next year, and 0.635 the third year, what was their average winning record for the three years?
.674 average

If they excluded the score of the second year, and averaged only the first and third years, what would their average winning record have been?
.641 average

Page 18

Decimals
Multiplication

Name ______________

Bicycle Data

Dana had a three-speed bicycle. She noticed that the bike wheel went around fewer times in first gear with one turn of the pedals than with one turn in third gear. She read in her bike manual that the gear ratio for third gear was 3.7, for second gear 2.5, and for first gear 1.4. The gear ratio is the number of turns of the wheel compared to the number of turns of the gear, or pedals. Multiply the circumference of her bike wheel by the ratio of the gear to find the distance traveled by her bike.

1. The circumference of Dana's wheel is 1.95 meters. She measured on the pavement to find out exactly how far the wheel had traveled in two turns of the pedals in third gear (ratio of 3.7). How many meters did it go?
   1.95 x 3.7 x 2 turns = 14.43 meters
2. Dana then measured to find out exactly how far the wheel had traveled in two turns of the pedals in second gear (ratio of 2.5). How many meters did it go this time?
   1.95 x 2.50 x 2 turns = 9.75 meters
3. Finally, she measured the distance her bike traveled in two turns of the pedals in first gear (ratio of 1.4). How many meters did the wheel go in first gear?
   1.95 x 1.4 x 2 turns = 5.46 meters
4. How much farther did the bicycle go in third gear for two turns of the pedals than in first gear for two turns?
   14.43 − 5.46 = 8.97 more meters
5. Dana measured the distance her bike traveled in third gear for 25 turns of the pedals. How many meters did the bike go?
   1.95 x 3.7 x 25 turns = 180,375 meters

Answer the following.

6. Dana and her next-door neighbor, Kathryn, rode their bikes 4.1 kilometers to a friend's pool to swim. How far did each go both ways?
   8.2 Km.
7. If they went swimming 6 days in the week, how many kilometers would each ride in a week?
   49.2 Km.
8. Will they have to turn their pedals more often if they are using first gear or third gear?
   They will turn more in first gear.

USE YOUR CALCULATOR
Dana rode her bike to Kathryn's house for 2 pedal turns in first gear, then 2 turns in second gear, and 2 turns in third gear. How many meters is it to Kathryn's door?
29.64 meters

Page 19

Decimals
Multiplication

Name ______________

Delivering Encyclopedias

Scott's big brother, Leon, works as a delivery person for an encyclopedia company. Answer each question below about his work.

1. A small box of books weighs 8.3 pounds. A large box weighs 3 times as much. How much does the large box weigh?
   A large box weighs 24.9 lbs.
2. When someone buys a set of encyclopedias, the books come in 7 large boxes and 3 small boxes. How much does the whole set weigh?
   174.3 + 24.9 = 199.20 lbs.
3. In five days last week, Leon drove an average of 46.5 miles each day. How many total miles did he drive last week?
   He drove 232.5 miles last week.
4. Leon uses his own van to make deliveries, and the company pays him $.30 a mile to cover expenses. How much money was paid to Leon for his travel expenses last week?
   He was paid $69.75 for travel.
5. The five grade schools in Scottsdale each ordered a new set of the encyclopedias. Using the weight from problem 2, calculate how many pounds of encyclopedias Leon delivered to the school warehouse.
   He delivered 996 lbs. of books.
6. The company awarded five unabridged dictionaries as a free bonus for ordering 5 sets of the encyclopedias. Each dictionary weighed 5.48 pounds. How much weight did the 5 dictionaries add to the delivery?
   The dictionaries weighed 27.4 lbs.
7. On days when he is not making deliveries, Leon works in the warehouse getting orders ready to ship out of town. One day he boxed 27 sets of encyclopedias. Using the weight from problem two, how much did the 27 sets weigh?
   The 27 sets weighed 5,378.4 lbs.
8. Leon took the 27 sets of encyclopedias to the shipper. He divided the load evenly for 3 trips. How many pounds did he carry in each trip? How many sets did he take in each trip?
   1792.8 lbs per trip 9 sets per trip

USE YOUR CALCULATOR
Leon makes $8.64 an hour for his delivery and packaging work. If he works 40 hours a week, what are his wages for the week?
He makes $345.60 /week.

Page 20

Decimals
Mixed Operations

Name ______________

Physical Fitness

The P. E. teacher at Marcy School was helping the children get in shape for the national fitness test. Read each problem and circle whether to add, subtract or multiply. Write the answer on the correct line.

1. Janet jogged 1 mile on Monday, 2.6 miles on Tuesday, 1.5 miles on Wednesday, 2.25 miles on Thursday, and 4.1 miles on Friday. How many miles did she jog this week?
   (Add) 11.45 miles Subtract ____ Multiply ____
2. Bart did 75 sit-ups every school day this week. How many sit-ups did he do this week?
   Add ____ Subtract ____ (Multiply) 375 sit-ups
3. Randy did .48 as many sit-ups as Bart. How many sit-ups did Randy do this week?
   Add ____ Subtract ____ (Multiply) 180 sit-ups
4. Marilyn can do 35 chin-ups without stopping. The next best person in the class can chin .60 as many times as Marilyn can. How many chin-ups can he do?
   Add ____ Subtract ____ (Multiply) 21 chin-ups
5. Ebony can run the mile in 9.75 minutes. Crystal runs the mile in 8.6 minutes. In how many fewer minutes can Crystal run the mile?
   Add ____ (Subtract) 1.15 fewer Multiply ____
6. Thomas is 5 feet 3 inches tall. The recommended weight for boys this height is 123.5. If Thomas weighs 126.8, how much weight should he lose before taking the national fitness test?
   Add ____ (Subtract) 3.3 lbs. Multiply ____
7. Deana jumps the rope an average of 85.6 times without stopping. Terri's average is 3.2 times Deana's average. What is Terri's average for jumping rope?
   Add ____ Subtract ____ (Multiply) 273.92

USE YOUR CALCULATOR
On the day of the fitness test, 156 students took the test. If .75 of them passed all the tests, how many students is that?
Add ____ Subtract ____ (Multiply) 117

Page 21

Fractions
Concepts

Name ______________

Story Problems

Ms. Jeffrey's class wrote math problems that show how to use fractions. Solve these problems.

1. A Clydesdale horse could weigh 1/2 a ton. If a camel weighed 900 pounds, which animal would weigh more?
   The horse weighs more at 1000 lbs.
2. It took Jeremy 20 minutes to do the dishes. His sister can do them in 1/4 of an hour. Who can do the dishes in less time?
   Jeremy's sister is quicker at 15 min.
3. A prize-winning tomato weighs 480 grams. A big, red onion weighs 4/10 of a kilogram. Which weighs more, the tomato or the onion?
   The tomato weighs 80 grams more.
4. Ian ate 1/4 of the pizza. Cory ate 1/5 of the pizza. Phillip ate 1/2 of the pizza. Who ate the most pizza?
   Phillip ate the most pizza.
5. Lupe's hamburger weighed 5/16 of a pound. Was it smaller or larger than a quarter-pound hamburger?
   Lupe's hamburger weighed more than 1/4 lb
6. Eric's shoe is 8 inches long. His brother Bobby's shoe measures 1/2 of a foot long. Which boy is probably older? Explain.
   Eric is probably older because his feet are 2 inches longer.
7. Their father's shoe measures 13 inches. Is their father's shoe longer or shorter than 1/3 of a yard?
   One inch longer than 1/3 yard
8. Jane measured 3/4 of a cup of milk. If her recipe called for 5/8 of a cup, should she add milk or pour some of it out of the cup?
   She needs to pour 1/8 of a cup out
9. Jackie took 13 minutes to braid her hair. Her mother takes 1/6 of an hour to comb her own hair. Which takes longer, Jackie's hair or her mother's hair?
   Jackie's hair takes 3 minutes longer.
10. Patty and Charles are reading the same book with 250 pages. Patty has read 1/2 of the book. Charles is on page 189. Who has read more of the book?
    Charles has read more.

USE YOUR CALCULATOR
Evelyn's dad owns an orchard with four kinds of fruit trees. 1/5 of the orchard is in pear trees. 5/100 of the orchard is in apricot trees. 1/2 of the orchard is in apple trees. The rest of the orchard is in peach trees. How much of the orchard is in peach trees? 1/4 of the orchard

Page 22

Fractions

Name ______________

Conversion

Calculate the number of units in each fraction described.

1. If there are 12 eggs in a dozen, how many eggs are in...
   - 1/2 dozen? 6
   - 1/4 dozen? 3
   - 1/3 dozen? 4
2. If there are 100 centimeters (cm) in a meter, how many cm are in...
   - 1/2 meter? 50
   - 1/4 meter? 25
   - 1/10 meter? 10
3. If there are 16 ounces in a pound, how many ounces are in...
   - 1/2 pound? 8
   - 1/4 pound? 4
   - 3/8 pound? 6
4. If there are 4 quarts in a gallon, how many quarts are in...
   - 1/2 of a gallon? 2
   - 1/4 of a gallon? 1
   - 3/4 of a gallon? 3
5. If there are 60 seconds in a minute, how many seconds are in...
   - 1/2 of a minute? 30
   - 1/4 of a minute? 15
   - 3/4 of a minute? 45
6. If there are 1,000 meters in a kilometer, how many meters are there in...
   - 1/10 of a kilometer? 100
   - 1/2 of a kilometer? 500
   - 1/4 of a kilometer? 250
7. If there are 30 days in most months, how many days are there in...
   - 1/3 of a month? 10
   - 1/6 of a month? 5
   - 1/10 of a month? 3
8. If there are 24 hours in one day, how many hours are there in...
   - 1/3 of a day? 8
   - 2/3 of a day? 16
   - 1/4 of a day? 6
9. If there are 36 inches in one yard, how many inches are there in...
   - 2/3 of a yard? 24
   - 1/4 of a yard? 9
   - 1/2 of a yard? 18
10. If there are 2,000 pounds in one ton, how many pounds are there in...
    - 1/2 of a ton? 1000
    - 1/4 of a ton? 500
    - 1/20 of a ton? 100

USE YOUR CALCULATOR
If there are 5,280 feet in one mile, how many feet are there in...
- 1/2 of a mile? 2,640 ft.
- 2/5 of a mile? 2,112 ft.
- 3/4 of a mile? 3,960 ft.

Page 23

Fractions
Concepts

Name ______________

Reduce It

Reduce each fraction in the sentences below to its lowest terms. Rewrite the sentence correctly on the line.

1. Daniel slept 8/24 of a day.
   Daniel slept 1/3 of the day
2. Emilia rides the bus to school 6/8 of the time.
   Emilia rides the bus to school 3/4 of the time.
3. Jim spent 5/25 of his dollar at the candy store.
   Jim spent 1/5 of his dollar at the store.
4. Josie completed 80/100 of her math problems correctly.
   Josie completed 4/5 of her math prob. correctly.
5. Amy scored 4/8 of the points in the soccer game.
   Amy scored 1/2 of the points in the game.
6. The sun was hidden by clouds 20/30 of the days in January.
   The sun was hidden by clouds 2/3 of the days
7. The cars raced 20/60 of the hour.
   The cars raced 1/3 of the hour.
8. The baby cried for 10/60 of an hour.
   The baby cried for 1/6 of an hour.
9. Of the students in Maureen's room, 8/24 have pets.
   Of the students in Maureen's room, 1/3 have pets.
10. Ethan drank 6/12 of the sodas in one day.
    Ethan drank 1/2 of the sodas in one day.
11. Of the students in the band, 4/16 played saxophone.
    Of the band students, 1/4 played saxophone.
12. 9/27 of the vehicles are trucks.
    1/3 of the vehicles are trucks.
13. In the lunchroom, a child drank 250/1000 liter of milk.
    In the lunchroom, a child drank 1/4 liter of milk.
14. 18/20 of the class will be in the holiday program.
    9/10 of the class will be in the holiday program.

USE YOUR CALCULATOR
The space shuttle was 8/1028 of its way to the planet Mars.
The space shuttle was 2/257 of its way to Mars.

Page 24

Fractions

Name ______________

A Trip to the Ocean

Maria's girls' club earned enough money from their cookie sale to have a camp-out at the ocean. Read about their trip and write your answers in complete sentences.

1. The bus started with 6 1/2 gallons of gasoline. When the driver added 9 1/2 more gallons of gasoline, how much gasoline did the bus have in it?
   The bus had 16 gallons of gas.
2. The girls and their leaders stopped for a picnic after driving 58 1/5 miles. After the picnic, they drove 43 4/5 miles before reaching the ocean. How far were they from home?
   They were 102 miles from home.
3. Before leaving home, they had made sandwiches for their lunch. They had 7 1/2 tuna sandwiches, 4 1/4 cheese sandwiches, 2 3/4 peanut butter sandwiches, and 5 1/2 beef sandwiches. How many total sandwiches did they bring?
   They brought 20 sandwiches.
4. The leader cut their watermelon into 16 slices for lunch. They ate 8 of the slices. What fraction of the watermelon did they eat?
   They ate half of the melon (1/2).
5. If they saved the rest of the watermelon for dinner, how much was left for their dinner?
   Half was left, or 8 slices.
6. When they arrived, they took 1 1/3 hours to set up the tents. They spent another 2/3 hour getting their bedrolls ready. How long did they work before they could play in the ocean?
   They worked for 2 hours.
7. The girls swam and played in the water for 1 3/4 hours. Then they sat in the sun for 3/4 hour. How many hours did they play and sun-bathe?
   They played and sun-bathed for 2 1/2 hours.
8. After dinner they had a camp fire. First, they sang for 1 1/3 hours. Then, they told ghost stories for 2/3 hour. If they put out the fire and went to sleep at 10:30, what time did they begin the campfire?
   They began at 8:30 pm.
9. The next morning, 3/8 of the girls went fishing. The rest of the girls hunted for shells. If there were 8 girls altogether, how many hunted for shells? How many went fishing?
   Five girls hunted for shells. Three went fishing.

USE YOUR CALCULATOR
The bus used 28 gallons of gasoline. If gasoline cost $1.19 per gallon, how much did they spend in all on gasoline?
They spent $33.32 on gasoline.

If that was 1/2 of the money they spent on the trip, how much did they spend in all?
In all, they spent $66.64 on the trip.

Page 25

Fractions

Name ______________________

Cooking for a Crowd

Amy and Gina helped their mother and father prepare the food for the party after their new baby brother's christening. Read about their day and answer the questions in complete sentences.

1. The recipe for crab dip calls for 3/4 cup of sour cream. Amy has a 3-cup container of sour cream. Does she have enough sour cream to triple the recipe?
   She has enough to triple the recipe. 3/4 x 3 = 2 1/4
2. For the apple salad, they have cut up 6 1/3 cups of apples, 2 2/3 cups of celery, and 2/3 cup of nuts. How many cups must the salad bowl be able to hold?
   The salad bowl must hold 9 2/3 cups.
3. The girls put 1/5 of the grapes on a platter and 2/5 of the grapes in a basket. They put the rest in the refrigerator. What fraction of the grapes are in the refrigerator?
   2/5 of the grapes are in the refrigerator.
4. Gina put 32 slices of bread on the table. 1/2 of the bread is wheat bread and 1/2 is rye bread. How many slices are wheat bread?
   Sixteen slices are wheat bread.
5. Gina put 3/4 cup of mayonnaise into a bowl. Later in the party, she added 1/4 cup more mayonnaise. How much mayonnaise did she put out?
   She put out 1 cup of mayonnaise.
6. The girls put out 3 1/2 pounds of potato chips and 3 3/4 pounds of corn chips on the tables. How many pounds of chips did they put out?
   They put out 7 1/4 lbs of chips.
7. Mother made 8 1/3 quarts of lemonade and 9 5/6 quarts of tea for the guests. How many quarts of drinks did she prepare?
   She prepared 18 1/6 quarts of drinks
8. Their father bought a sheet cake decorated with the baby's name and the date. They cut it into 28 pieces. After the party, 4 pieces were left. What fraction of the cake was left?
   1/7 of the cake was left.
9. The baby received 14 gifts at the party. If Mother wrote 1/2 of the thank-you notes the next day, how many thank-you notes did she have left to write?
   She still has seven more to write

USE YOUR CALCULATOR

They used 3 1/2 bags of ice at the party. If each bag holds 100 cubes of ice, how many cubes of ice did they use?
They used 350 ice cubes.

Page 26

Fractions

Name ______________________

Love That Motorcycle

James loved to ride on his uncle's motorcycle. Read about his adventures and write the answers in complete sentences.

1. James and his uncle rode 9 3/4 total miles on flat and hilly country. 2 1/4 miles of their ride was on flat roads. How many miles did they ride in the hilly country?
   They rode 7 1/2 miles in hilly country.
2. Last week, his uncle took him to a spring festival in another town. When they began, the motorcycle's tank was full with 5 gallons of gasoline. When they got back, his uncle put in 2 3/4 gallons to fill it up. How many gallons did they not use?
   They didn't use 2 1/4 gallons.
3. The new helmet James's uncle bought for himself cost $54. He bought one for James for 1/2 as much. How much did the helmet for James cost?
   James's helmet cost $27.
4. His uncle gave him a ride to school one day. It is 4 1/10 miles from James's house to school. They passed Harold's house after 2 2/10 miles. How far is it from Harold's house to school?
   Harold is 1 9/10 miles from school.
5. The motorcycle usually holds 3 quarts of oil. One day, it developed a leak and only 3/4 quart of oil was left. How much oil had leaked out?
   2 1/4 quarts of oil leaked out.
6. James and his uncle went on a long trip to see James's grandmother. They stopped for breakfast when they had gone 1/5 of the way. They stopped for lunch when they had gone another 2/5 of the way. How much of the trip did they have yet to complete?
   They must still go 2/5 of the way.
7. James noticed that each 1/5 of the trip took them 1 hour. How many hours had they been traveling when they stopped for lunch?
   They had traveled for 3 hours.
8. How many total hours would it take them to drive straight to Grandmother's house?
   The whole trip to Grandmother's will take 5 hours.

USE YOUR CALCULATOR

James's uncle makes payments on the motorcycle. So far, he has paid for 1/4 of the motorcycle in 1 year. How many more years will he be making payments on the motorcycle?
He must make payments for 3 more years.

Page 27

Fractions

Name ______________________

Pleasure Boating

Gerald's dad has a boat store near a large lake. Read about the problems Gerald encounters. Write the answers in complete sentences.

1. Gerald's favorite boat at the store is 22 2/4 feet long. Another boat they sell is 5 1/4 feet shorter. How long is the second boat?
   The second boat is 17 1/4 feet long.
2. Gerald's dad usually spends about 1/2 of his working time in the store and 1/2 of his time in boats on the lake with customers. If Dad works 40 hours a week, about how much time a week does he spend in the store?
   He spends about 20 hours in the store.
3. Gerald and his dad took their boat out on Saturday for 3 hours. They spent 2 1/4 hours fishing. They rode around for a while before they went home. How long did they ride around?
   They spent 3/4 of an hour riding.
4. The anchor on the boat has 300 total feet of rope. 100 feet of the rope is cotton, and the rest is a special sturdy nylon rope. What fraction of the rope is nylon?
   Two-thirds of the rope is nylon (2/3).
5. The boat had 15 2/3 gallons of gasoline in it. When full, it holds 30 2/3 gallons. How much gasoline would fill it up?
   15 gallons would fill the tank.
6. Gerald had a rope which is 8 3/4 feet long. He used 6 1/4 feet to tie the boat to the dock. How much rope did he have left to coil neatly on the dock?
   He coiled 2 1/2 feet of rope.
7. Every spring, Gerald and his dad scraped the barnacles off the boat. It took them 8 3/4 hours this year. Last year it only took them 3 1/4 hours. How much longer did it take them this year?
   It took 5 1/2 more hours this year.
8. Sometimes they put the boat on a trailer and took it to another lake. It takes them 3 1/4 hours to get there. Once they had a flat tire after they had driven 1 1/4 hours. How many hours were they from the other lake?
   They were 2 hours from the other lake.
9. Their trip took them 4 3/4 hours. Since it usually takes 3 1/4 hours to get there, how long must it have taken them to change the tire?
   It took them 1 1/2 hrs. to change the tire.

USE YOUR CALCULATOR

Gerald plans to buy a boat when he is 20 years old. He thinks he will have lived 1/4 of his life by then. To what age does Gerald think he will live?
He thinks he will live to be 80.

Page 28

Fractions

Mixed Operations

Name ______________________

Paint, Plaster, and Other Problems

Patricia's mother runs a home decorating store. She helped Patricia write these fraction problems. Can you solve them?

1. Alice spent two days painting her bedroom. She painted 1 1/3 hours on Wednesday and 2 1/3 hours on Thursday. How many hours did she paint in all?
   She painted for 3 2/3 hours.
2. Mr. Lennett painted 3 rooms in his house. It took him 2 2/3 hours to paint the first room. The second room took 2 1/3 hours, and the third room took 2 hours. How long did it take him to paint 3 rooms?
   He painted 3 rooms in 7 hours.
3. Mr. Riley purchased 2 gallons of paint. If the hall took 1 1/4 gallons of paint, how much paint did he have left?
   He had 3/4 of a gallon left.
4. Patricia's mother had just tiled a kitchen floor. She put down 23 1/2 tiles on one side of the sink, and 37 3/4 tiles on the other side. How many tiles did she lay in all?
   She placed 61 1/4 tiles in all.
5. Carpet was on sale. On the first day, one roll of carpet started with 100 yards on it. They sold 29 3/4 yards in the morning and 32 1/8 yards in the afternoon. How much carpet was left from their 100-yard roll?
   38 1/8 yds. were left.
6. Mrs. Kester plans to wallpaper her kitchen and bathroom. The kitchen will take 56 2/3 square feet of wallpaper. The bathroom will take 31 1/3 square feet of wallpaper. How many feet of wallpaper should Mrs. Kester buy?
   She should buy 88 square feet.
7. Mrs. Kester will need 1 1/4 bags of wallpaper paste for the bathroom and 2 3/4 bags for the kitchen. How many bags should Mrs. Kester buy?
   She should buy 4 bags.
8. Mrs. Kester bought material for new drapes. She bought 27 1/2 yards for the living room curtains. She needed 14 1/4 fewer yards for the dining room curtains. How many yards did she need for the dining room?
   She needed 13 1/4 for the dining room.

USE YOUR CALCULATOR

Patricia helped her mother with the tile job. She was paid $25 for her work. She made 1/4 what her mother was paid. How much was her mother paid?
Her mother made $100.

Page 29

Fractions

Mixed Operations

Name ______________________

State Trivia Game

When Mrs. Campbell's class studied about their state, they wrote questions about the state involving fractions for a game. Answer their questions in complete sentences.

1. In 1850, there were about 6 1/2 million pine trees in our state. Most of the pine trees were cut down for lumber early in this century. Now about 1 1/3 million pine trees exist in the state. About how many pine trees were lost?
   About 5 1/6 million pine trees were lost.
2. Our state has two major cities. City A has 4 1/2 million people. City B has 3 1/6 million people. How many more people does city A have than city B?
   City A has about 1 1/3 more people.
3. Many of the people in our state work in auto manufacturing. Company A employs 1/2 as many people as company B. If company B employs 50,000 people, how many people does company A employ?
   Company A employs 25,000 people.
4. The students in Mrs. Campbell's class decided that 1/4 of the time it is too hot in their state, and 1/4 of the time it is too cold. How much of the time is the temperature just right?
   Half of the time the temp. is just right
5. Our state has many rivers and parks. About 1 4/12 million people go camping each year. About 9/12 million people go canoeing each year. How many more people camp than canoe?
   7/12 million more people camp.
6. Of all the cities in the state, about 1/3 of them have a population under 25,000. What fraction has a population over 25,000?
   Two-thirds of the cities have pop. over 25,000.
7. During the Ice Age, a glacier covered about 3/5 of our state. About how much of the state was not covered by a glacier?
   Two-fifths of the state was not covered.
8. A major river is about 2,400 miles long in total. About 1/6 of the river runs through our state. How many miles of the river run through our state?
   Four hundred miles of the river run through the state.

USE YOUR CALCULATOR

Our school has about 450 students. Our students represent about 1/1000 of the elementary school students in the state. About how many elementary school students are in our state?
There are 450,000 elementary students in our state.

Page 30

Fractions

Multiplication

Name ______________________

Stump the Teacher

The students in Mr. Davidson's class were playing "stump the teacher." See if you can solve their problems.

1. If baseball cards are worth 1/10 of a dollar each, how much are Brad's 54 cards worth?
   $5.40 for 54 cards
2. If 6/8 of Sally's 8 puppies are female and 1/2 of the female puppies have been sold, how many female puppies have been sold?
   3 female puppies
3. Felipe used 2/3 cup of cheese for each pizza. If he made 4 pizzas, how much cheese did he need to buy?
   2 2/3 cups of cheese
4. There was 3/4 of a cherry pie in the refrigerator. If Sue ate 1/3 of that, how much of the total pie did she eat?
   She ate 1/4 of the pie.
5. Francis bought 15/16 of a yard of fabric. She used 1/2 of it to make a dress for her doll. What fraction of a yard did she use?
   She used 15/32 of a yard.
6. If a lot is 5/8 of an acre, and the house covers 1/2 of it, what fraction of an acre is covered by the house?
   The house covers 5/16 of an acre
7. At the track fair, I entered 5 sprint contests. If each race was 1/4 mile long, how many miles did I sprint in all?
   1 1/4 miles in all.
8. The class had 1/4 of an hour to take a math quiz. Nate used only 1/3 of the time. What fraction of an hour did Nate use for the quiz?
   Nate used 1/12 of an hour.
9. Sally and Kim live 3/8 of a mile apart. If they each walked 1/2 of the way and met in the middle, what part of a mile did each walk?
   They each walked 3/16 of a mile.
10. This year's summer vacation was 1/6 of the year. How many months long was the summer vacation this year?
    2 months
11. Paul's dog was asleep 2/3 of the day. How many hours was it awake?
    awake for 8 hours
12. The principal divided a bulletin board into thirds. He used 1/3 of 2/3 of the bulletin board for bus schedules. How much of the total bulletin board was used for bus schedules?
    He used 2/9 of the total board.
13. The art teacher gave Saul 1/2 of a bottle of glue. He used 3/4 of the glue. What part of the whole bottle of glue was left when he was done?
    1/8 of a bottle was left.

Page 31

Fractions

Multiplying Mixed Numbers

Name ______________________

Cooking Conversions

Beth and her mother were cooking a birthday dinner for Beth's father. They were serving fresh pasta with chicken and mushrooms for ten people. The recipe served only four people. They multiplied each ingredient by 2 1/2 to get the correct amount. Read each recipe ingredient and write the amount they will use on the line.

1. 1/4 pound of butter — 5/8 of a pound of butter
2. 1/3 cup of flour — 5/6 cup of flour
3. 2 1/2 cups chicken stock — 6 1/4 cups chicken stock
4. 3/4 cup cream — 1 7/8 cups cream
5. 1/4 cup wine — 5/8 cup wine
6. 2 teaspoons salt — 5 tsp. salt
7. 1/4 teaspoon pepper — 5/8 tsp. pepper
8. 1 cup sliced mushrooms — 2 1/2 cups mushrooms
9. 6 mushroom caps — 15 mushroom caps
10. 1 cup cooked ham — 2 1/2 cups ham
11. 1/2 pound pasta dough — 1 1/4 pound pasta dough
12. 2 cups cooked chicken — 5 cups chicken
13. 1/3 cup grated cheese — 5/6 cups cheese

For dessert, they made an apple tart. Convert the recipe for four people to amounts for ten people.

1. 1/2 pound butter — 5/4 → 1 1/4 pounds butter
2. 1 cup brown sugar — 2 1/2 cups brown sugar
3. 3 cups apple slices — 7 1/2 cups apple slices
4. 1/4 cup almonds — 5/8 cup almonds
5. 2 teaspoons lemon juice — 5 tsp. lemon juice
6. 1/4 teaspoon cinnamon — 5/8 tsp. cinnamon
7. 1 1/4 cups flour — 3 1/8 cups flour
8. 1 teaspoon sugar — 2 1/2 tsp sugar
9. 2 eggs — 5 eggs

Page 32

Measurement

Metric Length

Name ______________________

How Far? How Long?

Ms. Martinez made this sign about metric length for her class. Refer to the sign to answer the questions below.

1 kilometer = 1000 meters 1 meter = 100 centimeters 1 centimeter = 10 millimeters	km = kilometer m = meter cm = centimeter mm = millimeter

1. Eric can throw a ball about 2,300 cm. How many meters can he throw the ball?
   23 meters
2. Barbara's book is 30 mm thick. How many centimeters thick is the book?
   3 cm
3. Delores can reach 2 meters high. How many centimeters can she reach?
   200 cm
4. Holly can take a giant step of 960 mm. How many centimeters can she step?
   96 cm
5. We walked 3,000 meters in the shopping mall. How many kilometers did we walk?
   3 km
6. Rae Ann is 1,540 mm tall. How many centimeters tall is she?
   154 cm

Circle the answer that makes the most sense.

1. On our trip downtown and back, we drove the car 40 ______.
   mm cm m **(km)**
2. A city block is 120 ______ long.
   mm cm **(m)** km
3. My 8-year-old sister, Diana, is 143 ______ tall.
   mm **(cm)** m km
4. Rodney has a handspan of about 14 ______ wide.
   mm **(cm)** m km
5. A fly has a wingspan of about 8 ______ wide.
   (mm) cm m km
6. An acorn is about 1 ______ wide.
   mm **(cm)** m km
7. A drinking fountain is about 1 ______ high.
   mm cm **(m)** km

Page 33

Measurement

U.S. Customary Length

Name ______________________

Football Team Workout

As Ms. Parrish's class watched the high school football team, they wrote these math problems about the team and the field. Refer to the chart to answer the questions below.

1 mile = 1760 yards 1 mile = 5280 feet 1 yard = 36 inches 12 inches = 1 foot	mi. = mile yd. = yard ft. = foot in. = inch

1. Jo Anne's brother threw the ball 27 yds. How many ft. did he throw the ball?
   81 ft.
2. The football field was 100 yds. long. How many ft. long was the field?
   300 ft.
3. The football field was 162 ft. wide. How many yds. wide was the field?
   54 yds.
4. The team missed a first down by 1/3 of a yd. How many in. was that?
   12 in.
5. The football is 11 in. in length. At least how many footballs would have to be placed end to end to equal more than a yd.?
   4 footballs
6. The pass receivers practiced 40 yd. sprints. How many feet did they run each time? How many inches?
   120 feet, 1440 inches

Circle the answer that makes the most sense.

1. A baseball bat is about 3 ______ long.
   inches **(feet)** yards miles
2. A ball point pen is about 6 ______ long.
   (inches) feet yards miles
3. A stepladder is about 6 ______ tall?
   inches **(feet)** yards miles
4. The distance around a large pond is about 3 ______.
   inches feet yards **(miles)**
5. A bathtub is about 1 ______ wide.
   inch foot **(yard)** mile

Page 34

Measurement

Metric Capacity

Name ____________

How Much? How Full?

Jana and her friends wrote some problems about capacity in metric terms. Refer to the chart to answer the questions below.

1 kiloliter	=	1,000 liters
1 liter	=	1,000 milliliters
kl	=	kiloliter
l	=	liter
ml	=	milliliter

1. Jana found that the fish tank held about 20 liters of water. How many milliliters of water did it hold?
   20,000 ml
2. Her teacher asked her to give the fish some vitamins each day. If she gave them 35 milliliters each day, how many milliliters would she give them in a week (Monday through Friday)?
   175 ml
3. Terri waters 6 plants in the classroom. She gives each of the plants 500 milliliters of water. How many milliliters of water does she need to water all of the plants? How many liters does she use?
   3,000 ml , 3 liters
4. Susan took 5 milliliters of cough medicine 4 times a day for one week. How many milliliters of medicine did she take in a day? In seven days?
   20 ml/day 140 ml/week
5. A truck brings fuel oil to school which is stored in a 12-kiloliter tank. How many liters does the tank hold when it is full?
   12,000 liters

Circle the answer that makes the most sense.

1. A drop of water is about 1 ______ of water.
   (milliliter) liter kiloliter
2. A water cooler holds about 15 ______ of water.
   milliliters (liters) kiloliters
3. A milk transport truck tank holds about 12 ______ of milk.
   milliliters liters (kiloliters)
4. A single can holds about 340 ______ of soda.
   (milliliters) liters kiloliters
5. A bucket of paint holds about 4 ______ of paint.
   milliliters (liters) kiloliters

Page 35

Measurement

U.S. Customary Capacity

Name ____________

Liquid Refreshment

Kerri is in charge of the fruit punch at the PTO thank-you tea. She has only a one-cup measure. Using the chart, help her change the recipe to cups.

1 gallon = 4 quarts 1 quart = 2 pints 1 pint = 2 cups 1 cup = 8 ounces	gal. = gallon qt. = quart pt. = pint oz. = ounce c. = cup

1. The recipe calls for 2 quarts of water. How many cups of water should she use?
   8 cups of water
2. It calls for 16 ounces of frozen lemonade and 8 oz. frozen orange juice. How many total cups of lemonade and orange juice are in the recipe?
   3 cups
3. The water and frozen juice are mixed with 2 quarts of pineapple juice. How many cups of pineapple juice will she mix in?
   8 cups pineapple juice
4. Next, she must add 4 quarts of ginger ale. How many cups are in 4 qts.?
   16 cups
5. How many cups of carbonated water should she add if the recipe calls for 2 quarts?
   8 cups
6. Finally, 2 cups of sugar are added to the mixture. How many total cups of ingredients have been used in the punch?
   (43 cups + 2 cups sugar) 45 cups
7. Kerri added ice and poured the punch into 4 1/4-quart pitchers. If each person at the tea was served about 1/2 cup of punch, how many people will this recipe serve? (Remember, the sugar dissolves.)
   about 86 people

Circle the answer that makes the most sense.

1. A can of motor oil is about 1 ______ .
   cup pint (quart) gallon
2. A glass of orange juice is about 1 ______ .
   (cup) pint quart gallon
3. A large bucket of paint is about 1 ______ .
   cup pint quart (gallon)

Page 36

Measurement

Metric Mass

Name ____________

How Much Does It Weigh?

The students in Mrs. Penny's fifth grade classroom brought in a collection of things to weigh. Using the chart, answer the questions below.

1 kilogram = 1,000 grams 1 gram = 1,000 milligrams	kilogram = kg gram = g milligram = mg

1. Beverly brought a tennis ball to school. If it weighed 60 grams, how many milligrams would 3 tennis balls weigh?
   180,000 mg
2. Aaron brought a can of chicken soup that weighed 360 grams. Would 3 cans of soup weigh over or under 1 kilogram?
   over 1 kg (1080 g)
3. Rachel brought a troll doll that weighed 100 grams. About how many from her collection would make a kilogram of troll dolls?
   10 dolls
4. Steven's hair comb weighed 35 grams. How many mg does his comb weigh?
   35,000 mg
5. Emily brought a peanut that weighed 8 grams. How many grams would 100 peanuts weigh?
   800 g
6. One of Harold's shoes weighed about 500 grams. How many kg would both of his shoes weigh?
   1 kg

Circle the answer that makes the most sense.

1. A city phone book probably weighs about 2 ______ .
   milligrams grams (kilograms)
2. A medium-sized apple has the mass of about 175 ______ .
   milligrams (grams) kilograms
3. A postage stamp probably has a mass of 50 ______ .
   (milligrams) grams kilograms
4. A chalkboard eraser has a mass of about 50 ______ .
   milligrams (grams) kilograms
5. A new pencil weighs about 5 ______ .
   milligrams (grams) kilograms

Page 37

Measurement

U.S. Customary Weight

Name ____________

Vegetable Stand

Cary worked at the farmer's market last summer, weighing and selling fruits and vegetables. Using the chart, answer the questions below.

1 ton = 2,000 pounds 1 pound = 16 ounces	ton = t. pound = lb. ounce = oz.

1. Cary's father drove a truck to the farmer's market that could carry 2,000 lbs. of fruits and vegetables. How many tons could his truck carry?
   2,000 lbs = 1 ton
2. Green beans were $1.19 per pound. If a woman bought 4 pounds, how much change would she get back from a $5 bill?
   $.24 change
3. One man bought 1/2 pound of endive. How many ounces did he buy?
   8 oz.
4. Cary's dad had a special on cantaloupe at $.25 per pound. Cary's friend bought 2 cantaloupes. If his total was $1, how many pounds of cantaloupe did he buy?
   He bought 4 lbs.
5. On Saturday, Cary gave away a free recycling sticker for every customer who brought their own bag. He gave away 263 stickers. If the average customer who recycles buys 4 pounds of produce, how many pounds of food did they probably sell?
   1,052 lbs of food
6. Cary's dad recently put a new top and cover on the stand. The top and cover weighed 1/2 ton. How many pounds did the top and cover weigh?
   1,000 lbs.

Circle the answer that makes the most sense.

1. A rhinoceros may weigh 2 ______ .
   ounces pounds (tons)
2. A bowling ball weighs about 16 ______ .
   ounces (pounds) tons
3. A regular sack of flour weighs 5 ______ .
   ounces (pounds) tons
4. A baseball weighs 5 ______ .
   (ounces) pounds tons

Page 38

Measurement

Temperature Celsius

Name ____________

Weather Forecast

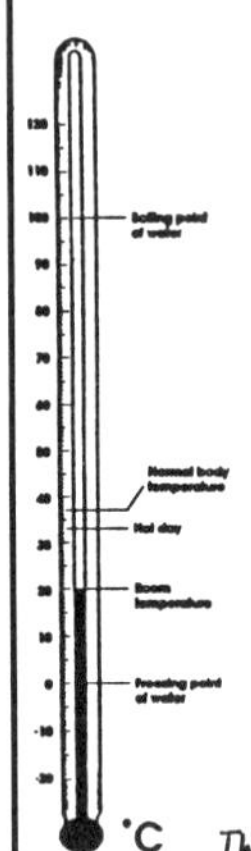

Karla did her science fair project on weather forecasting. She recorded the temperature daily in degrees Celsius. Answer her questions in complete sentences.

1. The average temperature in January was 10°C. The average temperature in February was 6°C higher than in January. What was the average temperature in February?
   The average temp in Feb. was 16°C
2. It was cold enough for Karla to go ice skating outside on January 24. Did she record the temperature as -15°C, or 15°C?
   It was -15°C, below freezing.
3. Karla filled a hot water bottle with boiling water to take along to warm her hands while she skated. When she started, how many degrees higher was the water in the bottle than the temperature outside?
   The water was 115° warmer.
4. What clothing should Karla have worn outside when the temperature was -15°C? She should wear coat, mittens, hat, boots, etc
5. One day, Karla had a body temperature of 40°C. Was she well or sick?
   She was sick
6. The average temperature in March, according to Karla's weather station, was 22°C. Using the temperatures from problem one, what was the average temperature between January, February, and March?
   The average was 16°.
7. Karla read in the newspaper that the average temperature in her city for August was 32°C. How much higher was the average temperature in August than in January?
   The temp is 22°C higher than in Jan.
8. Karla's mother thought the refrigerator was breaking down. Karla used her thermometer to check the temperature inside the refrigerator. Should it have read -5°C or 5°C?
   The refrigerator should be 5°C.

Page 39

Picture Graph

Name ____________

After-School Activities

The school newspaper editors at Bluebird Lane School encouraged students to take part in after-school activities. They published this picture graph. Refer to the graph to answer each question.

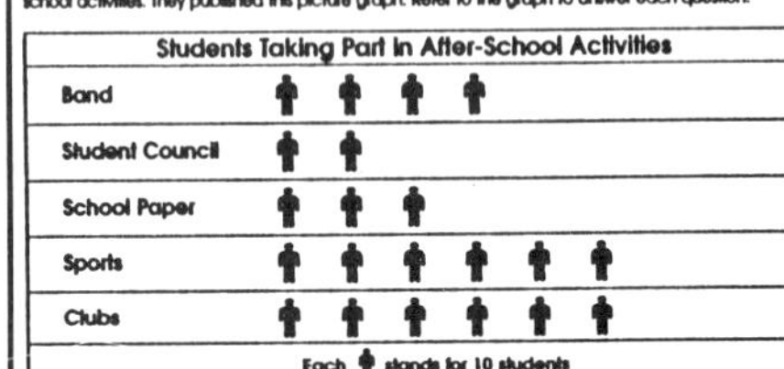

Bluebird School paper 1996 – (year will change)

1. How many total students take part in after-school activities?
   210 students participate.
2. In which two activities do the greatest number of students take part?
   Sports and clubs
3. How many more students take part in sports than in the band?
   20 more students
4. Which activity represented has the least participation?
   student council
5. How many fewer students take part in the student council than the school paper?
   10 fewer students
6. What is the title of the picture graph?
   Students Taking Part in After-School Activities
7. The picture graph should show when the graph was made and who made it. Please add "Bluebird School paper" and the current year to the bottom of the graph.

Page 40

Bar Graph

Name ____________

Vowel Search

Janet was helping out in the first grade. The children were learning to recognize the vowels. The children counted each vowel in a newspaper clipping. Janet made this bar graph to show the results. Refer to the graph to answer the following questions.

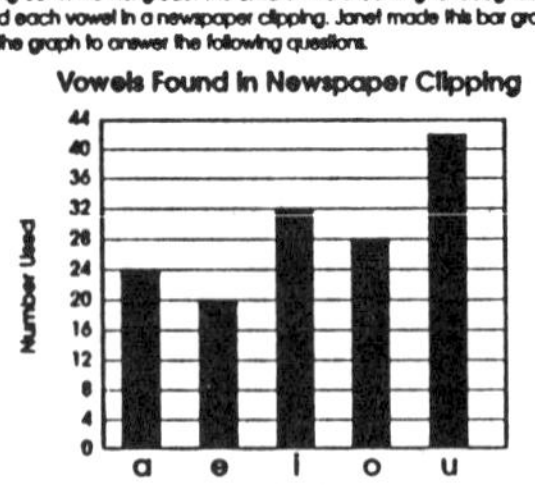

1. How many vowels did the children find all together?
   146 vowels
2. How many more times was "i" found than "e"?
   12 more times
3. How many fewer times was "a" found than "o"?
   4 fewer
4. What does it mean when the bar for the "u" stops between lines?
   The number falls between 40 and 44 (42).
5. On another paper, make a bar graph to show the number of times different vowels are used in your first, middle, and last name. Write two sentences that explain your graph.
   Answers will vary.

Page 41

Circle Graph

Name ____________

Ned's Allowance

Ned earned an allowance of $10.00 each week. He created this circle graph on his computer to show his parents how he spent it. Refer to the circle graph to answer each question below.

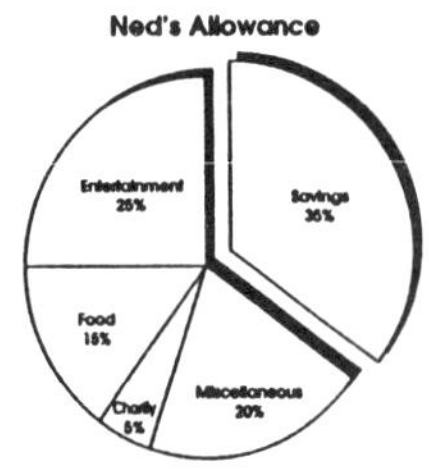

1. Ned highlighted the savings segment of the circle graph because his family believed that having a savings account was very important. If Ned saved $3.50 each week, how much would be left of his allowance for other things?
   $6.50 left after savings
2. Ned spends all of his entertainment allowance on movies. How much does he spend each week on movies?
   $2.50 on movies
3. How much does Ned spend each week on miscellaneous expenses? Name some things he might buy which would fall into this category.
   $2.00 Answers will vary.
4. If you have an allowance, create your own circle graph detailing your spending habits. If you don't have an allowance, write two sentences describing how you would spend $10.00 differently than Ned.
   Answers will vary.

Page 42

Line Graph

Name ____________

Library Lending Curve

While the local library was being remodeled last year from January to June, it was open only from 9 A.M. until 10 A.M. each day. The librarian prepared this line graph to show how many books were checked out during this period and after the remodeling was complete. Refer to the line graph to answer the questions below.

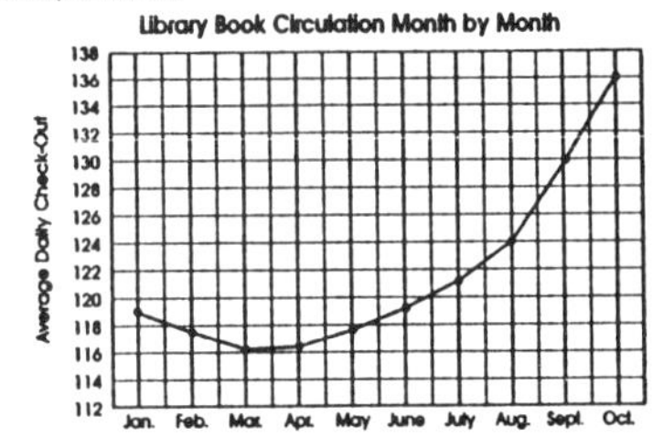

1. How many books, on average, were checked out daily in January? List the months that had a lower daily check-out rate than January.
   119 books/day; Feb., Mar., Apr., May
2. Were more books checked out from August to September or from July to August?
   August and September
3. Which two months had the greatest number of books checked out daily?
   September and October
4. What does it mean when a month shows a dot between the grid lines?
   The number falls between.
5. What is the average number of books checked out daily from January to October?
   122 books daily, on average

Page 43